THE
POWER
FIVE

THE POWER FIVE

A COOKBOOK

ESSENTIAL FOODS FOR OPTIMUM HEALTH

MICHAEL **CRUPAIN**, M.D., M.P.H.

NATIONAL GEOGRAPHIC

WASHINGTON, D.C.

CONTENTS

A DELICIOUS, HEALTHY COOKBOOK. CAN YOU DO THAT?

YOU MAY HAVE HEARD THE EXPRESSION "It's not brain surgery." Well, 16 years ago, when I was a young resident at New York Medical College, it actually *was* brain surgery. I frequently found myself standing over a patient's open cranium carefully sewing up their dura mater, a tissue paper–like covering protecting this vital organ. It required steady hands, technique, and years of study. Around that same time, you could also find me in the kitchen of David Bouley's Austrian restaurant, Danube, in Manhattan's Tribeca neighborhood. With the same meticulous attention and coordination (and usually a few bandages), I stood over a case of artichokes, carefully breaking down the heads by removing their thin, papery leaves, painstakingly peeling off any of the remaining fibrous outer layers with a paring knife to preserve the heart, the most precious part of the vegetable.

My life experiences tell divergent stories. I am a board-certified preventive medicine physician who rose through the ranks of Western medical schooling—first in neurosurgery and then in public health—to become a by-the-book wellness crusader with a personal mission to make the world a healthier place. That is the version of me who peers over the dinner table as a friend samples a spicy tuna roll and worries about the arsenic levels in the rice and the mercury in the tuna. (I never say anything in the moment because, hey, I'm not a jerk!) The other me is a cook and culinary expert, educated in my mother's kitchen since age three, and in the markets and villages perched on the rocky terrain of southern Italy, where a cooking instructor opened my palate to rich and rustic Italian pastas, calories be damned.

It was on my first trip to Puglia, while I was still a neurosurgery resident, that something clicked. I made a monumental decision to take a hiatus from my medical career to pursue more knowledge in the culinary world. In the end, the two sides of my identity collided: This cookbook tells that story.

In conceiving *The Power Five* I asked myself: "Can you really write a healthy cookbook—one that harnesses the power of food to boost vitality and longevity—with dishes that actually taste delicious?" The answer is yes—but it has taken me years of research, countless hours in the kitchen, and more than 900,000 Delta airline miles to perfect the recipes in this book to make that happen. My field study has been rigorous, yet delightful. I've tasted produce and talked with producers in farmers markets coast to coast, meandered through Middle Eastern food bazaars, dipped into bakeries in Paris, and toured dairies and fish farms in upstate New York. Now, I get to pass on everything I learned to you, including ways to maximize taste, texture, and presentation while extending your life and bringing you long-lasting health through the latest scientific research.

With each recipe, I also share a rich tapestry of characters I met along the way, from culinary professionals and luminaries who let me into their kitchens to ranchers, chefs, and grandmothers who shared secrets with me about finding and preparing the best ingredients on the planet. I have also spoken with dietitians, cardiologists, and top researchers who have dedicated their lives to decoding the foods our bodies need most to thrive. Their scientific vigor has illuminated the links among what we eat, how we feel, and how long we live.

As a cookbook collector, I find that very few of the glossy culinary chronicles I cherish could ever be marketed as healthy. "Diet cookbooks" are often, in fact, laced with strange ingredients, weird substitutions, and dishes that just don't taste all that great. The recipes in *this* book put flavor first and honor traditional cooking methods, resulting in mouthwatering meals no one will mistake for rabbit food.

The Power Five is about showing you how you can actually create more wholesome versions of the rich and hearty foods you love and introducing you to new favorites you've not yet dreamed of. The healthy component is largely a byproduct of utilizing the mightiest, most life-giving ingredients we have in the tastiest ways possible. *This, friend, is a cookbook that happens to be healthy, not a healthy book you can cook from.*

TAKING BACK THE POWER

Imagine a bustling town center, or piazza, filled with people, each one shouting nutritional advice at you—much of which is conflicting. It's a noisy spot and a confusing one at that. How do you know who to listen to? How do you know what will actually make a difference to your health and help you sidestep the most deadly diseases that rob us of living long and flourishing lives? That obstreperous scene is exactly where we find ourselves in the early 21st century. In the media and online, we are bombarded with a deafening deluge of "Eat *this now!*" and "Wait. No. *That* will kill you!"—making it hard to hear the really strong, science-backed facts whispered among the noise.

I recently came across the headline "The Deadliest Foods to Avoid," and I couldn't resist clicking. One of the tips was to avoid white flour altogether. Not a bad idea. But if you've ever gone to a grocery store, or attempted any sort of bread recipe, that advice can feel like a fool's errand. We're told to "eat more whole grains," but cooking or baking with them so they actually taste delicious—and are a worthy substitution for simple carbs—is no easy task. Showing you it's actually possible is one of the reasons I wrote this book.

Most of my professional journey has been charting the sometimes parallel, but often divergent, paths of the culinary and medical worlds. I have also traveled down the road of medical messaging in media, both as the director of food safety testing at *Consumer Reports* and on television as an on-air expert and behind-the-scenes advisor. The privilege of helping disseminate vital health information to the masses is a great passion of mine. But it has come with some lessons. The truth is that real science-based food advice isn't always that sexy. Much of daily life at a hospital is worlds away from the overly dramatic narratives of *Grey's Anatomy*. The best nutritional guidance isn't glossy enough for most TV shows, digital content, or magazines. The hunger consumers have for something new and different is insatiable. We are all clamoring for the next big thing or secret, which leads to clickbait health advice. But what if that bit of knowledge has been hiding in plain sight all along?

Traditional foods, consumed by mankind for centuries, are actually the holy grail of longevity. But it turns out that finding an obscure ingredient that can be powdered, put in a pill, and sold on Facebook with huge promises and phony celebrity endorsements is easier than getting people to sit down and eat some heirloom beans that are readily available at their local grocery store. The true superfoods are often the ones that were found in your grandmother's cupboard or garden.

I am a data person and have scrutinized hundreds of studies to assess what foods hold the power to give us what is most valuable—time—and narrowed them down to five. As Justin Timberlake promised to "bring sexy back" (although I have seen no quantifiable data that he actually did), I'm bringing superfoods back. This book harnesses the five most powerful foods on the planet, proved to help you live longer, in delicious recipes that are worthwhile competition to those quick-fix "miracle" supplements.

In 2017, one of the top googled words in America was "keto." While everyone was distracted by the bacon-friendly diet wave making loud headlines, a much quieter nutrition story went virtually unnoticed. A study that came out that same year by Renata Micha, R.D., Ph.D., from Tufts University's Friedman School of

Nutrition Science and Policy examined the cumulative effects of diet on the big killers: heart disease, stroke, and diabetes. What they found was that nearly half of all deaths from these conditions are linked to poor diet. In other words, nearly half of all deaths from these modern-day killers are preventable.

Findings like that should have stopped us in our tracks, but they're less "sexy" than fad diets. Why? Maybe we just don't know how to unleash the flavor of superfoods to make them craveable and attention grabbing.

None of us should be living in fear at every bite or, conversely, forcing something down because it's supposed to be healthy. We all want to do the best for ourselves and our families, but no one actually *wants* to eat the supposedly "better for you" option. It can be enough to make us throw up our hands and just order the cheese fries. That's where this cookbook comes in. I not only curated the most up-to-date and accurate evidence-based information on what specific foods are powerful enough to change the course of our lives; I also took on the challenge of cooking them up in the most enticing ways.

So let's get to it.

THE POWER FIVE TO STAY ALIVE

1. The Fruits & Vegetables
2. The Beans
3. The Grains
4. The Fish
5. The Nuts & Seeds

In this book, you'll find insight into the health benefits of each of these Power Five foods and learn how they work in your body to ward off disease. Then, you'll learn how to make and prepare them with mouthwatering recipes. Most of these recipes are simple and straightforward, with few ingredients, but there are also some that are more of a project, and that is by design. The point is to reimagine these key ingredients and learn how to make them a delicious part of your daily routine.

FIVE STRATEGIES FOR GETTING THE MOST OUT OF THIS BOOK

Now it's your turn to dive in. You can tackle this book cover to cover or choose your own adventure, jumping around to whichever recipes tickle your taste buds most. However you choose to begin, the following tips will help ensure you're making healthy habits a permanent part of your table.

1. **Follow the instructions, as written, the first time.**
   As the popular saying goes, "Learn the rules like a pro, so you can break them like an artist." I want you to experiment, substitute, and play with these recipes, to leave your mark on them. But first you have to master the techniques. Doing so will only make your future improvisations better. Use the recipe tips as your guide as you customize the recipes moving forward.

2. **Seek out the best ingredients you can find.**
   Ingredients don't have to be the most expensive, but they have to be the freshest. That means choosing in-season produce. Most of the ingredient lists in *The Power Five* recipes are relatively short, by design. I don't want them to feel intimidating or overwhelming. If you're not yet a regular at your local farmers market, give it a try; you'll find the highest-quality ingredients while supporting your local economy.

3. **Believe in recipe equality.**
   When I'm cooking with the Power Five foods, I don't spend too much time thinking about whether a dish is a main course or a side; each of the dishes gets equal real estate on my plate. I love cooking multiple dishes from this book for the same meal, sort of like beloved Israeli breakfasts, which are typically a smorgasbord of Power Five foods. This guarantees variety in your diet and has the bonus benefit of being impressive if you are cooking for friends and family. It's a great way to meal prep. Cooking a bunch of dishes at once makes for individual leftover meals that are delicious at room temperature and will save you time in the long run.

4. **Look for the Power Five badges.**

   These ingredients go really well together, so it was a challenge to decide which chapter each recipe belonged in. The solution was to call out the Power Five foods with badges so that you can note at a glance which groups star in each recipe. These badges will help you load up on the Power Five foods with every meal.

5. **The Power Five foods should make up the bulk of your diet.**

   The Power Five is not one of those restrictive diets peddling waist-slimming results in exchange for chewing cardboard. It's actually not a diet at all. You can certainly eat outside of these five food groups—in fact, I even provided a few recipes for meat and dessert! But the Power Five foods should be the pillars of your meals to get the most health benefits. Save the other stuff for special occasions or to have as smaller accompaniments to these dishes.

PART ONE

THE POWER FIVE

These five essential food groups will help you live longer and better. And here's why.

CHAPTER ONE

WHY FIVE?

THE NUMBER FIVE HAS A LOT OF POWER in our collective psyche. Most mammals have five fingers and five toes on each appendage; we have five senses; there are five basic tastes (sweet, salty, sour, bitter, and umami—more on that later); and the number five is a recurring theme in multiple religions. Now you have the Power Five foods, derived from decades of research into the ways the foods we eat can affect how our bodies fight off disease.

At Tufts University's Friedman School of Nutrition Science and Policy, a trailblazing study found that we Americans, as a nation, are *undereating*. Yes, undereating. Most doctors say our overeating of salt, processed meats, and sugar-sweetened beverages is responsible for our growing waistlines. They're not wrong, but the groundbreaking news is that our underconsumption of specific foods could mean the difference between life and death.

The Tufts researchers concluded that many of the more than 700,000 deaths from heart disease, stroke, or type 2 diabetes every year could have been avoided with the addition of fruits and vegetables, nuts and seeds, whole grains, fish, and vegetable oils into diets. And these dietary factors accounted for an ever-greater fraction of deaths among African Americans and Hispanics, who—due to a wide range of systemic inequalities—have had less access to fresh fruits and vegetables.

Let's put this into perspective: 700,000 deaths is more than 11 Soldier Field stadiums full of people dead—many of whom could have stayed alive if only they had eaten (or had more access to) more of the Power Five foods. Without question, four of the Power Five foods come from this research (vegetable oils, specifically olive oil, are already incorporated as heroes in every recipe in the book).

A large portion of our discussion of diet in this country centers on what we can't eat, shouldn't eat, or need to consume *less* of, but I believe there's enough evidence to reframe the conversation to what we should be eating *more* of. Imagine going to your doctor and instead of a lecture on cutting back, they encourage you to add more whole foods to your diet. It would be a game changer for many who feel weight-shamed or judged at the doctor's office. Instead, they'd be able to walk away feeling empowered and armed with useful knowledge.

A friend recently told me that the healthiest she's ever eaten in her life was when she was pregnant. I asked why she didn't adhere to all the tropes about overindulging on "pickles and ice cream" and "eating for two." She said that for the first time in her life, she was less focused on what she couldn't eat and paid more attention to what her body (and the baby) needed. She became a nutrient hunter, scouring her fridge and cabinets with a nutritional checklist to get enough of what was critical for the baby's proper development. After filling up on the nutrient-dense stuff, there was hardly any room to overindulge in fried, salty, and sweet snacks—and her palate eventually adjusted to crave the good stuff, anyway.

This nutrient-dense approach is actually a way of life in many parts of the world, including in the blue zones, five distinct areas on the planet where people live the longest, healthiest lives. It's from the blue zones that we get our fifth member of the Power Five: beans. I've had the pleasure of meeting Dan Buettner, the National Geographic Explorer and founder of Blue Zones, who has unveiled these region's dietary secrets. Dan found patterns in the diets across each of the blue zones, and consumption of beans is an irrefutable one. They're a keystone in every longevity diet in the world: lentils, garbanzos, and white beans in Sardinia, Italy; soybeans in Okinawa, Japan; black beans in the Nicoya peninsula of Costa Rica; butter beans in Ikaria, Greece; and a robust diet of lentils and other legumes in the Adventist community of Loma Linda, California.

People in the blue zones eat four times as many (or more) beans as the average American eats. And while living long is great, living well is best. The residents of the blue zones are proof of that—they live long, satisfying lives filled with delicious foods. The food on their plates is anything but bland. They are dining on herby lemon tabbouleh; gigante beans in savory tomato sauce; perfectly spiced sweet potatoes and lentils; flaky fresh fish; honey; sourdough bread; and *chanpurū* (a stir-fried tofu dish). Many even wash it all down with some good wine. With the most centenarians per capita on the planet in the blue zones, it's no wonder that residents make every moment count.

Many of the foods included in *The Power Five* are also associated with lower incidence of cancer. Research into the effects of food on cancer risk is complicated and inconsistent. I know people who eat very healthy diets (as do you), filled with fruits and leafy greens, who still got the dreaded diagnosis. It's not a cut-and-dry guarantee your smoothie and salad will keep you cancer free, but some of the data is very intriguing. A 2018 study led by researchers from Harvard T.H. Chan School of Public Health found that women who eat a high amount of fruits and vegetables every day may have a lower risk of breast cancer, especially aggressive tumors, than those who eat less. Their findings showed that cruciferous, yellow, and orange vegetables had a significant impact on breast cancer risk and that more was better; eating 5.5 servings proved more effective than 2.5 servings. Researchers at the National Cancer Institute at the National Institute of Health (NIH) have said, "People whose diets are rich in plant foods such as fruits and vegetables have a lower risk of getting cancers of the mouth, pharynx, larynx, esophagus, stomach, and lung." They also cite some evidence that suggests maintaining a diet rich in plant foods lowers the risk of colon, pancreas, and prostate cancers. What that tells me, as a doctor, is that creating habits of cooking and consuming vegetables can be beneficial in the long run, even if not a surefire bet against cancer.

Now, one may point out that a person regularly eating 5.5 servings of vegetables probably also exercises regularly and isn't smoking a pack a day. You can call that speculating or utilizing context clues, but the fact is, healthy habits beget other healthy habits, and that's what makes the difference. Eating the Power Five foods will help you feel better, have a more positive body image, and ultimately give rise to making healthier choices in your life. Is it the foods or other healthy habits associated with eating a better diet that ward off disease? It's not worth waiting for the jury to return an ultimate verdict; you might as well pick up as many health-giving habits as you can now and live the longest and best life you can.

You'll often hear the phrase "food is medicine," and it is. But, just like medication, food does our bodies no good if we forget to take it. So, instead of just saying that you need to eat more broccoli, I developed my Broccolini With Roasted Pepper Sauce recipe (page 79) so that you will actually *want* to cycle it into your weeknight menus.

Now, unless you thoroughly read the table of contents, which should have come with a spoiler alert, I have a surprise for you: There are actually seven chapters of foods in *The Power Five*. What gives? Well, while the Power Five foods are the pillars of health, I believe outright denying yourself the foods you desire the most will only send you on a craving spiral. (Cut to you doing donuts at the donut store drive-through.) Remember what I said earlier? This is not a restrictive diet but a habit-forming routine. It front-loads your plate with delicious nutrient-dense foods while allowing room to go outside the lines.

Instead of ignoring the undeniables—meats and sweets—I am giving you my favorite ways to prepare them, with healthier variations and tips that include thinking about what and where you buy ingredients. You'll see that alternative choices taste just as delicious.

And I don't expect you to form healthy habits alone in the dark. I've also put it all together in a power plan (page 241) that will make meal prep and menu planning easy enough to help you create new habits. This way you can ensure you're eating enough of the Power Five foods to reap their longevity benefits.

WHAT ABOUT DAIRY?

Dairy foods are rich in essential nutrients but can also be high in saturated fat. Some argue we aren't meant to consume milk because of its high lactose content, which many people can't tolerate. Interestingly, studies have suggested that dairy foods like milk, cheese, and yogurt may not increase the risk of heart disease. This may be because their other nutrients balance out the saturated fat. Having once produced a video blog called *The Dairy Show* (one of the first farm-to-table cooking shows about sustainable dairy farms and the products they make), I don't think you have to give up dairy. I choose fermented dairy foods, like labneh (page 28), which is the most traditional form. Studies of fermented dairy point to a potentially positive effect on cardiovascular health.

CHAPTER TWO

SOURCING INGREDIENTS

WHEN DEVELOPING THE RECIPES for this and my previous cookbook *(The What to Eat When Cookbook),* my team and I found again and again that higher-quality ingredients were easier to work with and yielded better-tasting food. I encourage you to seek out high-quality foods, but also sustainable ingredients, because what's good for the planet tends to be good for our bodies.

I don't share this to dissuade you from making do with the best versions of the Power Five foods that are readily available and are affordable for your budget. In fact, there are times when the simpler and often cheaper grocery store options work just as well. Frozen seafood, like the wild Alaska salmon sold in more affordable family packs at big-box stores, is often the best quality you can get. (In fact, most seafood at the counter of your grocery store has been defrosted, anyway.)

I'll share the secret to finding the best dried beans used by top chefs around the world, but I will also tell you, opening up a can of beans from the back of your cupboard makes little difference nutritionally to your heart, which will thank you kindly for your effort.

When it comes to ingredients, the source and quality matter. But that doesn't mean there's only one way to get the best nutrients and flavors. So here are the best practices for finding the best ingredients.

CHOOSE LSD: LOCAL, SEASONAL, DELICIOUS

No matter where I go—whether it's a new city in a new state or country—I always check where the farmers market is and make it my business to go see the local food offerings and cook with them. When I travel, I like to stay with people I know, and I have developed a reputation for trading a good home-cooked meal (and maybe even some new pots and pans) for a pillow.

When I'm in San Francisco, that means a trip to the Ferry Plaza Farmers Market. Three times a week, growers and vendors set up shop, showing off fresh dimpled berries, bountiful green peas and artichokes, and vibrant rainbow chard that looks like a cruciferous bouquet of leafy greens—all locally harvested. It's no wonder famed California chefs walk the stalls on the hunt for treasure. But you don't have to be a professional to enjoy the magic of a farmers market. When I'm home in upstate New York, I typically go to two farmers markets, one in Kingston and another in Rhinebeck. In between, I'll stop at farms and orchards along the way. Slow Fox Farm and the Montgomery Place Orchards Wayside Stand in Red Hook are favorites (legend has it that the latter is also Martha Stewart's favorite place to buy apples). More to the point: Rather than where I'm going, the key is what I'm going to these markets, farms, and stalls for. I'm interested in discovering what is in season. I'm obsessed with ingredients. Strolling past stalls full of the freshest, in-season produce inspires me to tinker and create in the kitchen. Finding the most interesting and delicious among the ingredients means I will be serving and eating the best-tasting and most nutritious meals.

I like to know where my food comes from and who is growing it. Eating is an emotional act, and knowing the people and story behind your food makes it taste that much more special. I share some of these stories in the recipes that follow—and I want you to write your own. Emphasizing the quality of ingredients is about encouraging you to take your own journey of appreciation, to discover local growers, farmers, and fishmongers near you. You will be surprised to see how much that knowledge and background will inspire you to increase how much of the Power Five foods you eat. So consider this your reminder to set your alarm and make a habit of shopping your local farmers market for the best of your region's in-season fruits and veggies.

ORGANIC PANIC

In a perfect world, all our food would be organic, and the right to eat produce grown without pesticides and meat raised without drugs wouldn't come with the hefty price tag. While grocery chains like Aldi are making an effort to offer organic food at a discount, it's still out of reach for most. Every grocery store run turns into an impossible choice between chemical exposure or financial burden. This leads many armchair experts to write off the benefits of organic food as marketing, and I don't blame them. After all, a lot of health halo labeling *is* just marketing. So, let's take two different approaches to the problem.

First, that of a health policy wonk, of which—let's face it—I am. Organically grown produce contains less cadmium, a toxic, naturally occurring metal in the soil, and less pesticide residue (though not zero, due to airborne spread from other farms). The good news for those who can't afford the price tag on organic fruits and vegetables: The regulated level of permissible pesticide residue on conventionally grown produce has been lowered.

Some data suggest possible health benefits of organic foods, when compared with foods grown by conventional processes. But there is limited information to prove how these differences can deliver overall health benefits. What is for certain is that it's better for the health of the amazing people who produce our food and for the environment in which our food is grown.

When it comes to nutrient levels, there are some small increases in organic produce, such as increased levels of some types of antioxidants and flavonoids. If I stayed in the lab or under the fluorescent lights of a cubicle, toiling away at data analysis, I might stop there. But I have gotten my boots wet at enough certified organic farms, dairies, and ranches to know that's not the full story. Organic meat, dairy, and eggs contain higher levels of omega-3 fatty acids, shown to greatly improve heart health and brain function. This has a lot to do with what the animals eat. And on organic farms, animals are fed a healthier, less additive-fueled diet. Cows, for instance, aren't given hefty portions of grain to increase their size right before going to market. That's why, when I do eat meat, I opt for grass-fed and grass-finished meats to garner the highest levels of heart-healthy fat. There's also the fact that certified organic farms are ecologically in balance with the planet in a way commercial farms are not, dumping fewer toxic chemicals into the air and soil that will eventually circle back to our bodies at some point.

But then there is the cook in me, who knows the real reason I choose organic is because if it's local, it just tastes better. Even the texture is superior in my opinion.

WHY DIY?

There are a lot of recipes in this book that call for items you may typically buy ready-made at the store: harissa, nut butter, yogurt, and sauerkraut, for example. I included recipes to make these in your own kitchens because it's often a cost-saver to make your own. And, in my opinion, there's really nothing better than making them from scratch—at least the first time. You will taste a difference and might adopt the DIY version as a standard part of your kitchen repertoire. That being said, I understand life is busy, so feel free to reach for the store-bought kind when making the *The Power Five* recipes if you're crunched for time. The recipes in this chapter are referenced throughout this book and are delicious staples to keep on hand.

FIVE LABELS TO DECODE

WHOLE FOODS

100 Percent Organic: This label can be used on certified organic fruits, vegetables, eggs, meat, or other foods, although you may simply see just the word "organic." On multi-ingredient foods, this label is only used if all of the ingredients, except for salt and water, are certified organic. An important note: Many farmers practice organic techniques but choose not to become certified because of the high cost of doing so. Finding an organic farm makes it easy to know right away that they are following the rules. For those not certified, you will have to get to know them and decide for yourself.

PACKAGED FOODS

Organic: While whole foods can just say "organic," packaged foods have percentages. Products with this label must have at least 95 percent of their ingredients be certified organic. The items that aren't organic must be from a United States Department of Agriculture (USDA)–approved list of additional ingredients. But it's important to note that while "organic" is meaningful on whole foods, on packaged foods it doesn't necessarily mean they are healthy. After all, they can be filled with organic sugar and organic white flour.

Made With Organic: These foods use at least 70 percent certified organic ingredients based on USDA guidelines.

Organic Ingredients: These products contain some organic ingredients, but less than 70 percent of the ingredients are organic.

Natural: This is what some call a "health halo," and it's kind of a lousy label. It's not regulated like "organic," and it has a malleable definition that's at the discretion of the producer. Generally, it means that the product contains no artificial colors, flavors, or preservatives. This doesn't have anything to do with the methods or materials used to grow the ingredients.

PREP TIME: 4 DAYS

LABNEH

Labneh is a Middle Eastern yogurt that's creamy, lemony, and loaded with pro-biotic bacteria. Labneh is made by straining yogurt curds to rid them of most of the whey—which is why it's sometimes referred to as "yogurt cheese." The first time you make it, you'll have to add some store-bought labneh to get the right cultures into the milk. Pro tip: Middle Eastern grocers carry the best.

1 gallon grass-fed whole milk

¼ cup store-bought labneh

Cheesecloth

1. Pour the milk into an Instant Pot, and cover with the lid. Using the yogurt setting, set the Instant Pot to high.

2. While the milk is heating, make an ice-water bath of equal parts ice and water in a metal bowl slightly larger than the inner pot. When the milk is done heating, remove the inner pot carefully and place it in the ice-water bath. When the milk drops below 115°F, skim off any film and whisk in the labneh. Return the mixture in the inner pot to the Instant Pot, and seal the lid. Change the yogurt setting to medium, and set the time to 15 hours.

3. Prepare a large mesh strainer by lining it with a cheesecloth or strong paper towels. Let the cloth hang over the edges of the strainer, and fold it over the edge. Place the strainer in the largest bowl you have that will hold it suspended above the bottom of the bowl.

4. Pour the contents of the inner pot into the strainer. Stir with a metal spoon to break up the curds. Cover the top of the lab-neh with the cheesecloth and a piece of plastic wrap. Drain the whey, and chill the labneh for 3 days. You will need to check the bowl after several hours and pour off the whey to ensure your strainer doesn't sit in a pool of it.

5. After several days, the labneh will stop losing whey and be significantly reduced in size. Store, covered, in the refrigerator for several weeks. Remember to always save ¼ cup to make your next batch.

ROSE HARISSA

Harissa is a spicy pepper condiment that has origins in Tunisia. Many premade versions are excellent, but I'd make water from hydrogen and oxygen if I could, because when you make your own, you know exactly what you're getting. So, this is my DIY version with healthy fats from olive oil and a nice dose of anti-oxidants from the peppers and spices. I especially like to use this as a quick marinade. Four guajillo chiles give me the heat level I like, a bit spicier than I've found in the commercial brands.

10 New Mexico or Anaheim chile peppers

4 guajillo chile peppers

5 sun-dried tomato halves in oil

1 teaspoon cumin seeds

1 teaspoon coriander seeds

1 teaspoon caraway seeds

3 cloves garlic

2 teaspoons rose petals

½ teaspoon smoked paprika

Zest and juice of 1 lemon

¾ cup olive oil

Salt

1. Cut the tips off the chiles, and shake out any seeds. Place the chiles in a 4-quart pot, and cover with water. Bring to a boil, turn off the heat, and add the tomatoes to the pot. Let sit for at least 1 hour. Make sure the chiles are fully submerged by placing a piece of parchment paper on top, followed by a small plate or bowl to weigh the chiles down.

2. Meanwhile, toast the cumin seeds, coriander seeds, and caraway seeds in a skillet over medium heat for 1 minute or until fragrant. Remove from the heat, and let cool. Then grind to a powder in a spice or coffee grinder.

3. When the chiles are fully rehydrated, drain, reserving the chiles, tomatoes, and ¼ cup chile water. Remove stems and any remaining seeds from the chiles (wear rubber gloves).

4. Process the garlic, rose petals, paprika, toasted spices, and reserved tomatoes in a food processor until minced. Add the lemon zest and juice, and pulse to combine. Add the chiles, and process until a mostly smooth paste is formed. If it's too dry, you can add 1 to 2 tablespoons of the reserved chile water. Gradually add oil through the food chute, processing into a thick paste. Season with salt to taste.

5. Transfer to an airtight container, and let stand to allow flavors to combine. Store in the refrigerator for up to 1 month.

PREP TIME: 15 MINUTES

TRAPANESE-STYLE PESTO

This pesto is traditionally made with fresh cherry tomatoes, but you can make a variation of it when cherry tomatoes are out of season using sun-dried tomatoes or semi-sun-dried tomatoes. I add a few sun-dried tomatoes here, even when cherry tomatoes are in season, for a little extra umami.

1 pint cherry tomatoes, halved

Salt

1 clove garlic

¼ cup toasted walnuts (or almonds—almonds are more traditional)

5 sun-dried tomatoes

1 bunch fresh basil

½ to ¾ cup olive oil

1. Season the cut sides of the cherry tomatoes with salt.

2. Pulse the garlic, nuts, sun-dried tomatoes, and a little salt in a food processor until combined. Add the basil, and pulse until chopped. Add the cherry tomatoes, and pulse to combine. Add olive oil, and pulse to combine. Season with salt to taste.

CAPER POWDER

I use capers packed in salt, but you can also use capers packed in brine. If you do use them in brine, you only need to rinse them, not soak them twice. Use this in my Roasted Cauliflower With Tomato and Caper Powders (page 63).

½ cup capers packed in salt

2 cups warm water

1. Rinse the capers thoroughly to remove excess salt. Put in a bowl, and soak in warm water for 30 minutes. Drain and repeat soaking.

2. Meanwhile, preheat the oven to 275°F. Line a sheet pan with parchment paper. Drain the capers, transfer to a paper towel to remove excess water (don't worry about getting them completely dry), and then place onto the prepared sheet pan.

3. Bake for 1 to 2 hours (depending on the size of your capers) or until the capers are dry and firm to the touch. If you see them develop a white coating, that's excess salt; take them out of the oven and rinse them in water, then return them to the oven to continue drying. Remove from the oven, and let cool.

4. Place the capers in a high-speed blender (such as a Vitamix). Process, gradually increasing the speed to high, until powdery.

ROASTED GARLIC AND CHERRY TOMATO SAUCE

This recipe is a back-to-basics staple you can use in so many other dishes or simply combine with whole wheat pasta, cooked in salty water, and enjoy! Cherry tomatoes have a perfect balanced flavor, and Sungolds are my favorite.

1 head garlic

3 pints cherry tomatoes (preferably Sungold), halved

¼ cup extra-virgin olive oil

Salt

1. Preheat the oven to 350°F. Line a baking sheet with parchment paper. Peel the outer husks from the garlic, but leave enough to keep the head intact. With a sharp knife, cut the top (stem end) off the garlic cloves. Wrap the garlic head in aluminum foil. Arrange the garlic and tomatoes in a single layer on the prepared baking sheet.

2. Roast for 1 hour. Remove from the oven, and let cool.

3. Place the tomatoes in a high-speed blender (such as a Vitamix). Unwrap the garlic, and squeeze the roasted cloves from their husks into the blender. Process, gradually increasing the speed to high, for 1 minute. Add the olive oil, and process for 30 seconds. Season with salt to taste.

TOMATO POWDER 🥄

The idea for this recipe came to me one late summer day when I came across some bright and cheery Sungold tomatoes at their peak. Sungold tomatoes are sweet cherry tomatoes with an inviting tangerine hue. Use this in the Tomato Semi-Cured Slow-Roasted Steelhead Trout recipe (page 175).

1 pint cherry tomatoes (preferably Sungold), halved

Kosher salt

1. Preheat the oven to its lowest temperature, around 175°F to 200°F. Arrange the tomatoes, skin sides up, on a parchment paper–lined sheet pan. Season lightly with salt.

2. Bake for 12 to 18 hours or until the tomatoes are shriveled and dehydrated. They may be a little soft when you take them out, but they will become crisp as they cool. Let the tomatoes cool completely at room temperature.

3. Grind the cooled, dehydrated tomatoes in a coffee grinder until it's a fine powder (30 seconds or longer).

WHIPPED TAHINI

4 cloves garlic

Juice of 1 lemon

1 cup tahini

Salt

1. Process the garlic in a food processor until chopped. Add the lemon juice, and pulse to combine. Let stand for 15 minutes. Drain the lemon juice from the garlic, and discard. Add the tahini to the garlic in the food processor, and pulse to combine. The tahini sauce will likely become very thick. With the food processor on, add ½ cup ice-cold water very slowly through the food chute until the mixture becomes airy. Season with salt to taste. Store in an airtight container in the refrigerator for up to 2 weeks.

AQUAFABA AIOLI

¼ cup aquafaba (liquid reserved from canned chickpeas)

1 tablespoon lemon juice

1 tablespoon Dijon mustard

1 clove garlic, chopped

1 teaspoon salt

1 cup neutral oil, such as grapeseed or extra-virgin olive oil

1. Process the aquafaba, lemon juice, mustard, garlic, and salt with an immersion blender for 2 minutes or until combined and frothy. Gradually add the oil, processing until a thick sauce forms.

MIXED NUT BUTTER

8 ounces walnuts

8 ounces pecans

8 ounces cashews

8 ounces peanuts

2 teaspoons flaxseeds

1 tablespoon honey

Salt

1. Process the walnuts in a food processor until a thick paste forms, about 3 minutes. Add the pecans, and process until incorporated. Add the cashews and peanuts, and process until a smooth paste forms. This will take 8 to 10 minutes. At first, you will have a chalk-like paste that forms a large ball in the food processor. Continue processing, and it will smooth out into a butter-like consistency. Add the flaxseeds and honey, and process to combine. Add salt to taste. Store in an airtight container in the refrigerator.

CORN BUTTER

There is a lot you can do with this sauce, including mixing it with pasta, serving it as a topping for grilled fish, smearing it on a piece of bread, or even chilling it and eating it like pudding. I like to serve it with roasted oysters (see page 181).

4 ears corn, shucked

Salt

2 tablespoons olive oil

1. Cut the corn kernels off the cobs. Cook the kernels in a cast-iron skillet over medium heat for 5 minutes or until fragrant and starting to soften, but don't let them brown.

2. Puree the corn in a high-speed blender (such as a Vitamix) until silky smooth. (This will take 3 to 4 minutes, and you may need to add 1 to 2 tablespoons water if it gets too thick.) When the corn butter is at a super-silky, velvety consistency, season with salt to taste, and blend in the olive oil. The corn butter will thicken further as it cools, so you will need to stir it before using, and you may need to add a little water to loosen it up.

CULTURAL APPRECIATION

Throughout this book, you will find stories about and nods to the many different cultures whose cuisines have inspired me as a cook. Within *The Power Five* recipes, I want to observe and salute how cultures around the world have found ways to make these five superfoods delectable. It's important to highlight the context of the dishes and techniques that are generations old—sometimes dating as far back as ancient times. We should celebrate the history and traditions that have shaped our shared palates. From Italy to Israel, my travels around the world have deeply influenced the dishes I share in these pages. Even my small hometown in New Jersey inspired one of my favorite recipes in this book, Chickpea Murphy (page 107).

My absolute favorite thing to do as a cook is to seek out grandmothers who will teach me their secrets; there is no better instructor on this planet than a grandma in the kitchen. My teachers—*nonnas, abuelas, grammies,* and *halmoni*—have shown me that within their rich culinary heritages are secrets to how to season and prepare the Power Five foods in ways that have been lost in our modern fast-food world. What's more, these grandmothers aren't begging their families to eat their food—they're barely keeping up with the demand as their hungry kin wipe their plates clean at family events. It goes without saying: We can learn from and adopt their wisdom.

A few years ago, before I traveled to Tepoztlán, Mexico, to spend New Year's Eve with a friend and his family, I spent time studying recipes from both the Hispanic and Indigenous cultures of that region. Learning from different cultures has opened my eyes to nontraditional preparations of some seriously healthy foods. In Mexico, that was *pipian,* a mole sauce made from toasted pumpkin seeds. On a recent solo trip to Jerusalem, I pulled up a stool at a bar called DKL. The bartender invited me to try their tasting menu. Now, it may have been the arak (a Middle Eastern distilled alcohol) talking, but I fell in love with a dish you would never find on a typical American menu: cured shrimp with yogurt. (Not to mention a surprise to find shrimp on a menu in Jerusalem.) The yogurt, of course, was labneh, and it proved my suspicion that in this corner of the world, the uber-strained version of yogurt goes on everything. The extra straining (even more than in Greek yogurt) makes labneh high in protein and chock-full of important micronutrients like calcium. If yogurt could go on shellfish, it certainly can make grilled stone fruit extra indulgent (page 55) and entice even the most salad-averse eater to dig into a bowl of tomatoes (page 83).

CHAPTER THREE

TURNING THE TIMETABLES

BOTH TIME AND FOOD HAVE FASCINATED ME for many years (in fact, some friends in high school nicknamed me Dr. Clockworks—a story for another day). I first became interested in the intersection of time and eating as a neurosurgery resident, when I began intermittent fasting without even trying. I was so busy, I only had time to eat one meal a day! Turns out, I was—involuntarily—onto something. Since then, a lot of science has emerged showing the importance of not just what you eat but also *when* you eat it. This science is what led Dr. Mike Roizen, the chief wellness officer emeritus at the Cleveland Clinic, and me to write our books *What to Eat When* and *The What to Eat When Cookbook,* both rooted in the scientific principle that keeping our meals in sync with our circadian rhythms is the best practice to improve our health. What this means is we should all try to eat with the sun: to eat more early and less later. Bottom line: Your largest meals should be earlier in the day, and dinner should be the smallest. The practice has helped me and countless others improve our health without feeling deprived. And in *The Power Five,* I return to the subject of time again—but not to give you a lesson in chrono-nutrition. Instead, I want to help you use time to your advantage in the kitchen when cooking with the Power Five foods.

First, let's talk about one of my favorite measures of time: the seasons. I'm obsessed with cooking with seasonal foods. Just like I try to consume most of my calories in a limited window of the day, I also try to eat certain foods only in the windows when they're at their peak. Things like ramps, asparagus, snap peas, peaches, plums, fresh tomatoes, and pears are reserved for the spring, summer, and fall, respectively. This helps me appreciate how special these ingredients are, and I look forward to the time when they're most delicious every year. Eating with nature's calendar is also a great way to save time, because when ingredients are at their best, they require less fuss in preparing them. That is why so many of the recipes in this book—like Summer Fruit Salad (page 59) and Boiled Cicoria (page 87)—are so uncomplicated.

Now, I have to admit, eating only what's in season isn't practical or entirely healthy. In places that have cold winters, the prospect of surviving on roots and tubers for four months—or longer—is downright depressing. (Trust me, I've tried. Some great things have come out of it, though, like the radish salad on page 77.) After a few weeks, my cravings for antioxidant- and fiber-rich greens like broccoli and Swiss chard have me buying produce shipped from across the country at my local supermarket. And that is absolutely okay, especially since certain fruits and vegetables do better than others. Fresh tomatoes are best eaten straight from the vine, but leafy greens, cucumbers, and cruciferous vegetables hold up well even after taking a road trip from one coast to another.

Another way to master time and food is to preserve your local produce when it's at its peak so that you can use it even when it's out of season or nowhere to be found. Without going as far as canning your own produce, there are simple things you can do, without much equipment, to preserve the bounty of the seasons. This was the inspiration for the oven-dried Tomato Chips (page 93) and Tomato Powder (page 33), which both make use of preserved tomatoes. You'll find other recipes to help convert ingredients with a short shelf life into something that can last much longer, including the sauerkraut recipe (page 61) and the labneh recipe (page 28), which converts perishable milk into longer-lasting yogurt.

THE FIFTH FLAVOR: UMAMI

Japanese scientists discovered umami, the fifth basic flavor, in 1907. (The other basic flavors are sweet, salty, sour, and bitter.) *Umami* translates to "savory," and the flavor is derived from three compounds naturally found in plants and meat: glutamate, inosinate, and guanylate. My Tomato Powder (page 33) is a great way to add umami and depth of flavor to all of your cooking. It's also easily stored in a jar in your cupboard so you can have it on hand, whether or not tomatoes are in season.

There is one more way we bring time into the equation in *The Power Five,* and that is in the time it takes to cook our foods. This book has plenty of recipes that can be made in a flash, but others rely on slow cooking to help bring out deeper flavors. In one recipe, Fennel Cooked to Death (page 60), the longer cook time brings out the sweetness in the stalky vegetable, which surprisingly contains no added sugars. Bonus: Fennel's high soluble fiber content may even help regulate insulin levels. That's worth clocking! And the incredible, simple roasted cabbage (page 91) will make you rethink everything you thought you knew about cabbage, using one important ingredient: time.

While a long cooking time does have the potential to destroy some nutrients, it can also enhance the value of some ingredients and make them more digestible. Take beans, for example. Cooking beans helps break down both lectins and the polysaccharides that cause gas and helps garner the most nutrition from them. And, while I love a raw tomato, a cooked tomato has higher levels of lycopene, an antioxidant that helps protect your heart and reduces the risk of cancer.

The time we spend cooking something, fast or slow, also changes the textures of foods. This is worth mentioning because time and again, I am told mouthfeel is one of the biggest barriers to entry for people when it comes to foods like vegetables. No offense to your parents or middle-school cafeteria chef, but I blame them for turning some of the most powerful foods on the planet into mushy morsels. I promise to show you how to use cooking time to create the amazing textures that will have even the biggest vegetable skeptics asking for seconds. This includes both long and quick-fire cooking. After all, sometimes mushy can be turned into luxurious, such as in Spicy Green Beans Cooked Forever (page 86). And other times, vegetables prove they can be great when barely cooked at all or eaten raw, like in my Raw Asparagus Salad (page 69). My pasta recipes—yes, you can eat pasta!—are all about timing, too, and the power of harnessing the toothsome perfection of an al dente noodle.

Before you get cooking, here's my final thought on time: While you will find many quick weeknight dishes in *The Power Five,* some of these recipes are more technical labors of love. While Sheryl Sandberg popularized the expression "Done is better than perfect," there are times when taking your time and striving for the inverse can be really confidence boosting. Creating meals for family and friends is my love language. Presenting those I cherish most in this world with a creation made from scratch is how I show them I care. It's also invigorating to the surgeon in me to master each task and technique. That practice has helped me form a reverence for food and how it's prepared and has helped me avoid so much of the junk food that permeates the world today. I hope giving these labors of love a chance—and the time they deserve—does the same for you.

PART TWO

EAT MORE

Now it's time to get into the Power Five foods and how they help you stay alive—and live better. I'll unpack the science behind each of these five essential foods and arm you with recipes so you can unleash their nutritious benefits in the most delicious ways.

CHAPTER FOUR

THE FRUITS & VEGETABLES

WHAT IS A FRUIT ANYWAY? WHAT IS A VEGETABLE? It's produce existentialism even Sartre would find delicious! Despite what your grade-school teacher told you, the answers may not always be cut-and-dry. In fact, a chef, a farmer, and a botanist may all have different answers. Technically speaking, a fruit is defined as anything that contains the seeds of the plant. So, sure, a peach is a fruit. But if you've felt the tingle of a pepper seed hitting your tongue, you might be questioning everything. That's right! A pepper is a fruit, avocados are berries, and your life is officially a lie. The tomato had so much chutzpah, it went all the way to the U.S. Supreme Court to be declared a vegetable, though technically it's a fruit. Reputations are at stake. In modern America, veggies have earned a wholesome reputation, while fruits are banned by many devotees of magic-bullet diet culture—they're as feared as any other carb. In the end, do these distinctions even matter? When talking about maximizing the benefits of fruits' vitamins and minerals … the answer is no!

The U.S. Dietary Guidelines recommend that adults consume about five servings—see, there's that number five again!—of fruits and vegetables a day, divided between 1.5 to 2 servings of fruit and 2 to 3 servings of vegetables. A serving is considered to be the equivalent of one cup full. Unfortunately, only about 12 percent of people in the United States meet the daily recommendations for fruit, and only 10 percent meet the vegetable recommendation. That comes down to about 1 in 10 Americans undereating two of the most life-giving food sources we have. And it's even bigger than just us. The World Health Organization (WHO) estimates 1.7 million deaths worldwide are connected to not eating enough fruits and vegetables. They also attribute 14 percent of gastrointestinal cancer deaths, 11 percent of heart disease deaths, and 9 percent of deaths from stroke to insufficient fruit and vegetable intake.

FRUIT: MALIGNED AND MISUNDERSTOOD

Fruits may deliver fructose, a naturally occurring sugar, and taste so mouthwateringly good that they feel like an off-limits dessert that will cause you to gain weight—but that's only half the story. Fruits are also fiber-rich, nutrient-dense foods that actually help *decrease the* incidence of obesity. In fact, a peer-reviewed article in the journal *Nutrients* compiled a variety of studies, including randomized controlled trials, prospective cohort studies, and cross-sectional studies, to conclude there is actually a paradoxical effect that links not eating fruit and weight gain. Scientifically speaking, fruit doesn't automatically make you fat, but *not* eating fruit could! If you look at the nutritional value of fruit, you may start to understand why. A large pear has only 120 calories and 7 grams of fiber, a peach has about 60 calories, and an entire cup of blueberries has about 50. With stats like these, it's hard to overeat fruit. So I've reached across the grocery store aisles and created recipes featuring fruits and vegetables that go beyond what you're used to. Who said bipartisanship is dead?

VEGETABLES: ROOTED IN SCIENCE

On a day-to-day logistical front, vegetables are low-calorie, fiber-rich foods that keep us full, help food pass through our digestive tract, feed our good gut bacteria, and fuel our bodies. We should talk more about nutrient density when we talk about food. Nutrient density is the amount of beneficial vitamins, minerals, fiber, and other healthful substances per calorie of our food. So often, you'll see someone staring at the label of a food or googling it to find out about its macros—how much fat, carbs, and calories it contains. I am all for intentional eating and awareness of what we're consuming, but what if we shifted our mindset to ask different questions when choosing our food?

What if we looked at everything we can physically eat in a day like a carry-on suitcase? Time, energy, and our bodies' satiety keep us from just ingesting pounds and pounds of food—there's a limit to the number of calories you can, or should, consume. If you're an indecisive packer, like me (who knows what they'll want to wear three days from now?), and you want to avoid checked-bag fees, you better make sure that bag meets overhead compartment limits. So you choose what's most essential to take. It's the same with choosing your foods: Ask what foods are going to give you the most nutrient density in the smallest package. By example, just one cup of one of the best cruciferous veggies there is, broccoli, provides 77 percent of your daily vitamin K intake. And that cup of broccoli is only 30 calories—taking up very little room. To get the same amount of vitamin K from pretzels, you'd need to eat 362 airplane-size (one-ounce) snack bags. That takes up a lot of room, spacewise (you would need five carry-on bags, and no flight attendant is going to let you on with that). It also means consuming 38,000 calories from pretzels, versus the 30 calories in broccoli, to get even close to the same nutritional value. Now, pretzels may still sound better to some of you than broccoli—I forgive you, because you've yet to make my Broccolini With Roasted Pepper Sauce (page 79)—but after eating that many packets, you may be reaching for the green stuff. (By the way, broccoli is such a favorite vegetable of mine, I dressed up as a head of it for Halloween in 2021.)

One of the blue zones, sunny Loma Linda, California, is home to a large community of Seventh-day Adventists, who consider healthy living as one of their principles. Seventh-day Adventists are mostly vegetarians, and that—along with getting exercise and refraining from alcohol and smoking—is one of the reasons they live a decade longer than other Americans. The Adventist Health Studies are not stand-alone findings, either. Fruits and vegetables are at the very heart of the Power Five foods because there's endless data on how eating them (and eating a lot of them) is essential to longevity. In fact, there are more than 25,000 specific reasons why; that's how many chemicals, known as phytonutrients, are in fruits and vegetables (nuts and beans also have them). Phytonutrients are essential because they are one of the things that may help prevent disease due to their antioxidant properties.

Antioxidants are so powerful they really deserve their own super-hero franchise. I'm looking at you, Marvel. When they're released in the body, they get to work at cleaning up cells, ousting free radicals that damage cells and hasten aging. We'll get a little granular about antioxidants when we unpack the importance of beans in chapter five. But while we can't draw causational lines between fruits, veggies, and a "skip cancer" card, there's enough overwhelming evidence that they do play a part in warding off deadly illness. So much so that we should make eating more of them priority one.

Take another example: leafy greens, which are some of the most nutrient-dense, bioactive foods on planet Earth, chock-full of vitamins and minerals that our bodies need to function. Skimping on fruits and vegetables is like not putting oil in your car; eventually things will start to break down. A lack of folate (high in asparagus), for example, could lead to anemia, and too little potassium (Swiss chard is a great source) can cause an irregular heartbeat.

It's time we all get beyond the finger-wagging of our parents pleading with us to finish our veggies and take an in-depth look at the science behind how to reduce the incidence of disease and extend our lifespans with the green (and yellow and red and orange and purple) stuff. It pains me when vegetables become relegated to side dishes; they can and should be the centerpiece of the plate. Even in the syllabi at cooking schools, it's very telling that the list is short in the fruit and vegetable course offerings. But it doesn't have to be. Take one of my favorite restaurants, the aptly named Dirt Candy on

Manhattan's Lower East Side. There, chef Amanda Cohen playfully transforms humble vegetables into main courses that make you smile with delight because of their cleverness and taste. Her table-side robata-grilled sugar snap peas wrapped in yuba reminds me of eating Peking duck. In *The Power Five* recipes, we similarly play with color, texture, heat, and layers to make dishes so memorable they can be the centerpiece of your table.

FIVE WAYS TO MAKE VEGETABLES THE STAR OF A MEAL

Have you ever heard the phrase "Here for a good time, not a long time"? Well, this book begs to differ. In fact, vegetables can be the life of the party while extending your life! Here are five chef secrets to make vegetables the star of the meal:

1. **Tap into their hidden natural sugars, and don't forget the spices.**
   You can enhance the sweet flavor of all vegetables by roasting, searing, or grilling them. The heat caramelizes their natural sugars, and that means flavor. Give it a try with my Oven-Roasted Cherry Tomatoes and Peas (page 81). In that recipe, I slowly roast tomatoes to concentrate their sweetness and blanch peas to make their own sweetness shine. Spices also add flavor and do so without adding calories, which makes them a go-to for me. You'll find lots of spices throughout this book that you may not be familiar with—I encourage you to experiment with them. Spices are rich in phytochemicals that reduce inflammation and make them powerful in their own right.

2. **Glaze vegetables without adding animal fat.**
   Traditionally, glazing vegetables has meant using butter, but it doesn't have to anymore. In Gochujang-Glazed Turnips (page 68), you'll get the same glazed effect and a lot of flavor without using one stick of butter. Gochujang is a fermented chile paste concentrate that's a staple of Korean cuisine and will make the root vegetables dance upon your tongue.

3. **Stack them up.**

   My recipe for Tiella (page 75) takes inspiration from the tra-ditional Puglian meal named for the terra-cotta dish it was originally cooked in. There are as many variations of this recipe as there are towns in southern Italy. *The Power Five* version layers potatoes, squash, fennel, and tomatoes. This is a hearty dish that eats like a meal. In another equally hearty stacker, my version of eggplant parmesan (page 89), I cut out the breading and frying and instead roast thin slices of eggplant that are stacked as high as can be.

4. **Make them creamy.**

   My Miso "Creamed" Corn (page 80) is one of my favorite things to serve to guests in the summertime. People are always amazed that it contains no cream at all. I've devised a tech-nique using a corn broth enhanced with miso that creates a rich, silky texture and highlights the pure, sweet corn flavor.

5. **Redefine what a salad is.**

   Who said salad has to be made of lettuce? One of the reasons people undereat vegetables is because all they think about is large bowls of leaves. If that's not appetizing to you, you'll be happy to hear there's not one traditional lettuce salad in this book. Instead, you will find a wide selection of "salads," includ-ing one with a variety of radishes that is crunchy and refreshing (page 77).

YOUR STARTING LINEUP

If the Power Five foods were a baseball team, these phyto-nutrients would be the starting lineup:

Carotenoids: You can thank the carotenoid lycopene for giving the lovely red and pink hues to tomatoes, water-melons, and grapefruits. You also may have gratitude for their ability to lower the risk of prostate cancer. Another carotenoid—often found in carrots—may protect your eyes from developing cataracts down the line.

Ellagic Acid: Ellagic acid may lower inflammation and fight off cancer. It also may reduce obesity.

Flavonoids: Flavonoids may help reduce people's risk of asthma, certain types of cancer, and coronary heart disease.

Resveratrol: Hero enough for putting wine on health lists, resveratrol is a powerful antioxidant responsible for clean-ing out the free radicals from our bodies.

Glucosinolates: Not only do glucosinolates give vegeta-bles their flavor, but when we cook veggies, they are also transformed into compounds some believe can slow the development of cancer in our bodies.

Phytoestrogens: Phytoestrogens can lower the risk of endometrial cancer and bone loss in women.

GRILLED STONE FRUIT WITH LABNEH AND BASIL

This is the new peaches and cream. It's so simple and sweet, you won't be able to tell if this is a salad or a dessert. Who likes labels anyway? This marries the world of nutrient-rich stone fruits with my favorite fermented dairy: labneh, a Middle Eastern yogurt strained until it takes on the consistency of a soft cheese. The herbs enhance the dish with subtle notes of citrus and spice.

4 stone fruits, such as peaches or nectarines

Olive oil

Salt

½ cup labneh (store-bought or see recipe, page 28)

Chopped fresh basil or lemon verbena

1. Preheat a grill or grill pan to medium-high heat. Cut the fruit in half, and remove the pits. Rub each half with olive oil, and sprinkle with salt.

2. Reduce the grill temperature to medium. Place the fruit on the grill and cook, covered with grill lid, for 5 minutes per side or until the fruit cooks all the way through and has a warm, custardy texture. Gently remove the fruit with a spatula, and place it on a serving dish. Top each fruit half with 1 tablespoon labneh and desired amount of basil. Serve immediately.

PREP TIME: 30 MINUTES

PINK FENNEL SALAD

This recipe is in honor of my friend Kathy. Pink is her favorite color, and sharing images of nice things—but not actually giving them to her—is our inside joke. During the pandemic I developed this salad so I could send her this beautiful picture. You may find it unusual because it contains raw beets, but slicing them very thinly makes them both easy to eat and delicious. Beets are rich in nitrates and may help control blood pressure. Fennel is one of my favorite vegetables because it is crunchy, flavorful, and a good source of vitamin C and antioxidants. When you add in the oranges and the healthy fats from the nuts and olive oil, this salad isn't just pretty on your plate; it makes your insides look good, too.

1 fennel bulb

1 red beet

Salt

1 orange (your favorite type)

¼ cup chopped toasted hazel-nuts or walnuts

¼ cup chopped fresh mint

¼ cup extra-virgin olive oil

1. Wash and dry the fennel (sometimes fennel can have some dirt under the first layer, so check). Cut off the root and stems. Cut the bulb in half lengthwise. Using a mandoline (be very careful, and be sure to use the guard), slice the fennel bulb as thinly as possible so that you can make nice slices that hold together, and place them in a bowl. Peel the beet and slice on the mandoline as well. Place the sliced beets on top of the fennel and season with salt. This will start to draw some of the water out of the beets and dye the fennel pink later when you mix everything together.

2. Cut the top and bottom off the orange just down to the flesh. Then use your knife to cut off the peel. Slice the orange cross-wise into thin wheels. Squeeze juice from any pieces of left-over orange into the bowl with the fennel mixture. Add the orange wheels to the bowl, and season with salt. Let the salad sit for 10 minutes.

3. Add the nuts and mint, and mix the salad to combine. As you mix, the salad should turn pink. Taste and adjust salt as desired. Finish with your best olive oil.

PREP TIME: 30 MINUTES

SUMMER FRUIT SALAD

This salad is perfect for those who crave sweet-and-salty combo foods, and it can be served as a starter, side, or dessert. A pluot is a cross between a plum and an apricot, so it has a firm texture and an unmistakable apricot flavor, and it's perfectly in harmony with the other fruit in this bowl.

3 heirloom tomatoes

1 white or yellow peach

1 nectarine

1 pluot

6 albino strawberries, hulled (or use 1 small cucumber, seeded and thinly sliced lengthwise)

Salt

¼ cup fresh basil leaves, chopped (or use mint)

¼ cup olive oil

1. Core the tomatoes, and cut them into quarters. Cut each quarter into triangular chunks. Cut the peach, nectarine, and pluot into similar-size chunks. Cut the strawberries into very thin slices. Toss together all the fruit, and season with salt to taste. Let stand until ready to serve. Toss with the basil and olive oil before serving.

NOTE: If your fruit is not at peak ripeness, you can enhance the flavors by adding some lime juice and a little honey and even some grated ginger.

FENNEL COOKED TO DEATH

I love raw fennel salads, but this recipe goes the opposite way and cooks the fennel until it is almost unrecognizable.

3 fennel bulbs (about 3 pounds total)

5 cloves garlic, peeled and smashed

¼ cup olive oil, plus more for finishing

Salt

Juice of 1 lemon

1. Wash and dry the fennel (sometimes fennel can have some dirt under the first layer, so check). Cut off the root. Cut the fronds from the fennel, and save for another use. Cut the bulb in half lengthwise. Core the fennel, and cut the bulb crosswise into ¼-inch-thick slices.

2. In a large, heavy pan, stir together the fennel, garlic, oil, ¼ cup water, and a sprinkling of salt. Cook over low heat for 2 hours, stirring occasionally, until the fennel is soft and almost falling apart. As the fennel starts to caramelize and the pan becomes dry, deglaze with more water and scrape up any browning bits from the bottom of the pan. If you hear the fennel cooking loudly, you have turned up the heat too high and/or you have run out of water (so add more until the fennel is cooked to the desired consistency). Season with salt to taste, and drizzle with olive oil and lemon juice.

SAUERKRAUT

Sauerkraut is a nutritional powerhouse loaded with prebiotic fiber that supports a healthy gut as well as healthy probiotics. The one drawback is that sauerkraut is very high in sodium, so I always rinse it thoroughly before using, which greatly reduces the sodium. Traditionally, sauerkraut is made in a stoneware pot, but if you don't have one, it's easy to make in smaller quantities. You don't even need to add bacterial cultures, because they come from nature.

1 head green or red cabbage, quartered with root attached

½ tablespoon kosher salt per pound of cabbage

1. Slice off the pointed top of each cabbage quarter. Using the core as a handle, cut the cabbage into thin strips along a mandoline (be very careful, and be sure to use the guard). Once you get close to the core, discard it, and begin again with the remaining cabbage quarters.

2. Place the cabbage in a large plastic bag or bowl. Using very clean hands, massage the salt into the cabbage for 5 to 10 minutes or until it is very broken down and starting to give off water.

3. When the cabbage has given up a significant amount of water (sometimes massaging is not enough; it could take a few hours of sitting), transfer the cabbage and the water to large glass jars (like mason jars or a fermenting pot), and pack down with a wooden spoon until the cabbage is completely submerged. If you need more water, add filtered water mixed with 1 teaspoon salt per cup. Weigh the cabbage down with drinking glasses that fit through the mouths of the jars, and cover loosely with plastic wrap so nothing can get in the jars. Let ferment in a cool place for 2 to 4 weeks. You can taste it to decide when it's done. After the fermentation is finished, store, covered, in the refrigerator.

PREP TIME: 15 MINUTES   **COOK TIME:** 40 MINUTES

ROASTED CAULIFLOWER WITH TOMATO AND CAPER POWDERS

Consider this your sign from the universe that your cauliflower is ready to live a little. Roasting caramelizes all the nooks and crannies of the cauliflower, leaving a sweet base for the Tomato Powder and Caper Powder to punch up the flavors with some acid and umami notes.

1 head cauliflower, cut into florets

2 tablespoons extra-virgin olive oil, plus more to taste

¼ cup Tomato Powder (see recipe, page 33)

2 tablespoons Caper Powder (see recipe, page 31)

1. Preheat the oven to 400°F. Line a sheet pan with parchment paper.

2. Place the cauliflower and olive oil in a bowl, and stir to combine. Transfer the cauliflower onto the prepared sheet pan, and roast in the oven for 25 minutes.

3. Remove the cauliflower from the oven, and return it to the large bowl. Sprinkle the cauliflower with the Tomato Powder and Caper Powder, and stir until evenly coated. Return the coated cauliflower to the sheet pan, and bake for 15 to 20 minutes or until tender. Remove from the oven, toss with olive oil to taste, and serve.

BABY ARTICHOKES À LA BARIGOULE

I prefer to cook with baby artichokes because they are delicious and less likely to cut you while you're cleaning them. Artichokes are also rich in inulin, a fiber that feeds gut bacteria and can help you feel full. This is a classic French preparation, which I like to serve on top of a piece of fish, under a small serving of burrata on a special occasion, or as a side dish to anything.

Juice of 1 lemon

2 pounds baby artichokes

2 tablespoons extra-virgin olive oil, plus more for finishing

¼ cup diced carrot

¼ cup diced leek or shallot

¼ cup diced fennel or celery

2 cloves garlic, diced

1¼ cups dry white wine

Kosher salt

Fresh parsley, basil, or mint sprigs for garnish

1. Fill a bowl with cold water, and add the lemon juice. Clean each artichoke by cutting off the top one-third of each and removing the tough outer green leaves. Using a Y-shaped peeler, remove the outer layer from the base and stem. Slice the artichoke in half, and add it to the lemon water to keep it from browning. Repeat with the remaining artichokes.

2. Heat the oil in a saucepan over medium heat. Add the carrot, leek, fennel, and garlic, and sauté for 2 minutes. Drain the artichokes, and add them to the saucepan. Cook for 2 minutes, then add the white wine. Bring to a simmer, and cover the surface with a disc of parchment paper. Simmer for 30 minutes or until the artichokes are tender but not falling apart. Drain and season with salt to taste. Garnish with your favorite herbs, and drizzle with olive oil to taste.

Kohlrabi
Remoulade
(page 71)

Gochujang-Glazed Turnips
(page 68)

Raw Asparagus Salad
(page 69)

GOCHUJANG-GLAZED TURNIPS

These cruciferous roots are a great source of fiber and vitamin K (important for bone health and blood clotting). Glazing adds a glossy, flavorful, saucy sheen, an age-old trick to make turnips enticing. Using gochujang—a spicy, sweet, and salty fermented Korean chile paste—makes them luscious. I like to use one from White Rose Miso, which draws its sweet quality from fermented soy and malted grain.

3 large turnips, cut into 2-inch chunks

¼ cup plum vinegar

2 tablespoons olive oil

2 tablespoons gochujang

1 scallion, green part only, chopped

Black sesame seeds

1. Stir together the turnips, vinegar, olive oil, and gochujang in a 4-quart or smaller pot. Add 1½ cups water, or just enough to cover. Bring to a simmer and cook, stirring occasionally, for 30 minutes or until most of the liquid has evaporated and the turnips are cooked through but still hold their shape. Stir to glaze the turnips in the sauce. Serve hot, garnished with scallion and sesame seeds.

RAW ASPARAGUS SALAD

This salad harnesses the beguiling, earthy grassiness of slightly sweet, mildly bitter asparagus and its fantastic crunch. Look for thick stalks, because starting with pencil-thin asparagus will make your life a lot harder. No matter what size asparagus you use, you can't peel the whole spear, so here we dice it up and add it to the salad. This dish has a little miso for body, umami, and probiotic bacteria; sunflower kernels for some crunch and to help get those healthy fats and protein in your diet; and some nigella seeds for color and flavor.

1 pound asparagus

Salt

2 tablespoons raw sunflower kernels

½ teaspoon nigella seeds

1 tablespoon white miso

1 Meyer lemon, zested and 1 tablespoon juice

3 tablespoons extra-virgin olive oil

1. Break off the tough ends of the asparagus and discard. Wash and dry the spears. Using a vegetable peeler (a Y-shaped peeler works best), peel the asparagus into long strips and place in a bowl lined with a dry kitchen towel or paper towel. (It's best if you peel the asparagus with it resting on a cutting board or counter to maximize the number of strips you can get.) When you have peeled all you can from a spear, break off the tip and add to the bowl. Season with salt to taste. Chop the remaining asparagus into a fine dice; set aside.

2. Toast the sunflower kernels and nigella seeds in a small saucepan over medium heat until fragrant (about 1 minute). Let cool while you make the dressing.

3. Whisk together the miso and lemon juice in a small bowl; gradually add the olive oil, whisking until blended. Add the diced asparagus, lemon zest, and toasted kernels and seeds to the dressing, and mix to combine.

4. Remove the towel from the bowl with the shaved asparagus strips. Using a slotted spoon, add the dressed asparagus mixture to the bowl with the strips, and toss to combine. Transfer to a platter, and serve.

NOTE: Be sure to wash your asparagus well to remove any grit and sand. I like to soak it in a bowl with a few water changes.

SERVES 2 TO 4

PREP TIME: 20 MINUTES   **COOK TIME:** 1 HOUR

KOHLRABI MASH 🐟

Kohlrabi is a cruciferous vegetable heralded for its potential in warding off cancer. It's filled with vitamins and minerals, like vitamin C, the immunity-supporting superhero that dabbles in crime-fighting free radicals, and potassium, which helps pump life-giving blood around your body. But can it rival mashed potatoes? Now, that is heavy lifting! I guarantee no one will miss the spuds. I like potatoes, but when an alternative that's lower on the glycemic index (the measure of how much something can increase blood sugar levels) can do the job, why not go for it?

2 pounds kohlrabi, peeled and cut into large chunks

2 to 4 cloves garlic, unpeeled

⅓ cup plain Greek yogurt or labneh (store-bought or see recipe, page 28)

Salt

¼ cup extra-virgin olive oil

1. Preheat the oven to 400°F.

2. Place the kohlrabi and garlic on a baking sheet or roasting pan, and cover with foil. Roast for 1 hour or until tender, stirring the vegetables halfway through. Remove the kohlrabi and garlic from the oven, and let cool, uncovered, until you can handle them.

3. Peel the garlic, then place the garlic and kohlrabi in a heavy-duty blender. Process on low until broken down, and then increase speed to puree. Stop the motor and add the yogurt. Puree on high until very smooth. Transfer to a saucepan, and cook over low heat until hot. Season with salt. Serve topped with extra-virgin olive oil.

NOTE: If you want to make this vegan, replace the yogurt with olive oil and drizzle through the lid of the blender while the motor runs. Add just enough to make a smooth puree. Finish with additional oil.

PREP TIME: 30 MINUTES   COOK TIME: 10 MINUTES

SLIVERED SWEET POTATOES

Sage and sweet potatoes are one of those happy marriages that seems timeless and exciting simultaneously. Szechuan stir-fried potatoes can be found in the most authentic of Chinese restaurants here in America, so this recipe takes inspiration from that tradition and adds an Italian twist.

1½ pounds sweet potatoes

¼ cup extra-virgin olive oil

20 fresh sage leaves, coarsely chopped

2 cloves garlic, diced

1 tablespoon minced ginger

Salt

1. Julienne the potatoes by either using the julienne attachment on your mandoline (be very careful, and be sure to use the guard) or slicing by hand. Soak the potatoes in water for 30 minutes; drain well, and pat dry.

2. Heat the olive oil in a large sauté pan over medium-high heat. Add the sage, garlic, and ginger. Cook until fragrant (about 1 minute), and add the potatoes. Cook, stirring often, for 8 minutes or until the potatoes are just cooked through and still hold their shape. Season with salt to taste.

SERVES 2 TO 4

PREP TIME: 30 MINUTES

KOHLRABI REMOULADE

Kohlrabi is the cabbage family's kooky aunt. It's a cool-weather crop, so it's a great ingredient when fall and winter roll around. Its high fiber content (1 cup has around 20 percent of the daily recommended value) makes it a low-glycemic food that could increase satiety and even help with digestive issues. I like to serve this remoulade with fish or on its own as a snack.

1 kohlrabi, peeled

1 fennel bulb

1 tablespoon grainy French mustard

¼ cup labneh (store-bought or see recipe, page 28)

Zest and juice of ½ lemon

Salt and pepper

1. Julienne the kohlrabi and fennel by either using the julienne attachment on your mandoline (be very careful, and be sure to use the guard) or by slicing by hand.

2. Mix together the mustard, labneh, and lemon zest and juice. Add the vegetables, and stir gently to combine. Season with salt and pepper to taste.

THE FRUITS & VEGETABLES

PREP TIME: 30 MINUTES   **COOK TIME:** 10 MINUTES

POACHED LEEK SALAD
WITH SUNCHOKES ⬭ ⬭

This salad is designed to help make you feel full, so it's great as a starter to keep you from overeating or as a snack to ward off a case of the munchies. Leeks and sunchokes, sometimes known as Jerusalem artichokes, are rich in a type of fiber called inulin, a prebiotic that's a wonderful source of nutrition for your gut bacteria. These bacteria eat the inulin, creating short-chain fatty acids, which researchers believe send a signal to your brain to make you feel satiated. You can cook the leeks the day before and bring to room temperature before serving. The mélange is topped with brain-healthy walnuts and mint.

3 leeks

Salt

4 medium sunchokes

1 orange

1 lemon

¼ cup toasted walnut pieces

¼ cup extra-virgin olive oil

2 tablespoons chopped fresh
mint or parsley

1. Cut the root and dark green parts off the leeks and discard. Slice the leeks in half lengthwise, and wash thoroughly to remove any dirt, keeping the layers intact.

2. Bring a large pot of water to a gentle simmer and season with salt. Gently add the leeks, and poach for 8 to 10 minutes or until cooked through and tender when pierced with a knife. Drain and cool.

3. Peel the sunchokes, and julienne by either using the julienne attachment on your mandoline (be very careful, and be sure to use the guard) or by slicing by hand (about 2 cups). Supreme the orange and lemon by removing the peel and pith from each using a knife, then cut the citrus into segments by slicing between each membrane, holding the citrus over a bowl to collect any juices.

4. Add the citrus segments and sunchokes to the accumulated juices in the bowl, and season with salt to taste. Gently stir in the walnuts and olive oil.

5. To serve, arrange the leeks on a platter and top with the sunchoke mixture. Garnish with mint or parsley.

TIELLA

This dish is an example of how you can stack veggies—like they do in Puglia, Italy, where this dish hails from—to help make them an impressive star of the meal instead of just a side. Healthwise, it's a home run, with a mix of vegetables that deliver a myriad of benefits.

1½ pounds purple potatoes

2 pounds tomatoes

1½ pounds yellow squash

1 large fennel bulb

1 large onion

1 to 3 hot red chile peppers (optional)

4 tablespoons extra-virgin olive oil, divided, plus more for the baking dish and finishing

2 tablespoons fresh rosemary leaves, chopped

6 cloves garlic, finely minced, divided

Kosher salt

2 tablespoons fresh thyme leaves, chopped

1 cup fresh whole wheat bread-crumbs (or use panko)

1. Preheat the oven to 425°F. Cut the potatoes into ⅛- to ¼-inch-thick slices using a mandoline (be very careful, and be sure to use the guard). Place in a bowl, with enough water to cover the potatoes, until you're ready to assemble the dish.

2. Cut the tomatoes with a knife into ½-inch-thick slices. Cut the squash, fennel, and onion into thin slices using a mandoline or a sharp knife. If you're using peppers, cut them into thin slices.

3. Oil a 13-x-9-inch baking dish. Drain the potatoes, pat dry, and return to the bowl. Drizzle the potatoes with 2 tablespoons oil, then top with the rosemary and one-third of the garlic. Season with salt to taste and toss to coat. Place the potatoes in an even layer in the baking dish.

4. Place the squash, thyme, half of the remaining garlic, and the remaining 2 tablespoons oil in the bowl. Toss to coat, then season with salt to taste. Spread evenly over the top of the potatoes. Top with the peppers, onions, and fennel in even layers, and sprinkle with desired amount of salt. Top with the tomato slices, the remaining garlic, and a little more salt. Sprinkle with the breadcrumbs.

5. Bake for 1 hour 30 minutes or until the veggies are cooked through and the breadcrumbs are toasted. Most of the liquid will have evaporated, but there should still be some bubbling around the sides when it comes out of the oven. Let rest for 15 minutes to soak up all the liquid. Serve warm or at room temperature, topped with a little more olive oil.

PREP TIME: 30 MINUTES   COOK TIME: 10 MINUTES

SALAD OF FOUR RADISHES THREE WAYS

In the Northeast where I live, the winter farmers markets don't have the bounty of the summer, but there's a wide variety of radishes. I'm not talking about little breakfast radishes. These are big, daikon-style radishes in white, red, and purple, and—the most breathtaking of them all—watermelon radishes, which have a pop of magenta that just makes you smile when you slice into one. Radishes are cruciferous vegetables, which are known cancer-fighting foods. Here, they're sliced thin and served raw, cooked, and pickled.

½ cup plum vinegar

2 watermelon radishes, divided

1 white radish

Salt

1 red radish

1 purple radish

2 cups pea shoots

¼ cup extra-virgin olive oil

Pepper

NOTE: If your radishes are a little spongy, you can add them to some ice water to bring a little crunch back to them before you begin preparing this recipe.

1. Bring the vinegar and ½ cup water to a boil in a saucepan. Cut 1 watermelon radish into ⅛-inch-thick slices using a mandoline (be very careful, and be sure to use the guard). Once the vinegar mixture has come to a boil, turn off the heat, and add the watermelon radish slices. Let cool. (This can be prepared in advance and refrigerated. You will not need all the pickled radish for this dish; save them for adding to your avocado toast or other snacks.)

2. Cut the white radish into ¼-inch-thick slices using the mandoline, and season with salt to taste. Heat a cast-iron skillet over medium-high heat, and sear the white radish slices in the dry pan, flipping them once to get a little char on both sides. Remove the radish slices from the pan, and transfer them to a bowl so that they steam a bit and cool.

3. Cut the remaining watermelon and the red and purple radishes into thin slices using the mandoline, place in a bowl, and season with salt to taste.

4. Combine the salted radishes, cooked radish, and desired amount of pickled radish. Toss with the pea shoots, and drizzle with the olive oil. Arrange on a platter, and sprinkle with pepper.

THE FRUITS & VEGETABLES

PREP TIME: 30 MINUTES **COOK TIME:** 40 MINUTES

BROCCOLINI WITH
ROASTED PEPPER SAUCE

Broccoli was my favorite vegetable—until I met Broccolini. More slender and tender than its cousin, Broccolini packs in the nutrition and flavor but is much easier to cook. It's also more expensive, so you can use broccoli here (or any of your other favorite vegetables).

¾ pound red bell peppers

1 to 2 long hot red chile peppers

1 tablespoon capers (preferably packed in salt)

6 large cloves black garlic, peeled (or use 6 cloves garlic, roasted)

½ cup kalamata or similar pitted olives

¼ cup extra-virgin olive oil

Kosher salt

2 bunches Broccolini (or use 1 head broccoli, cut into florets)

¼ cup walnuts, toasted (optional)

NOTE: You can roast the Broccolini instead of blanching, if desired. Preheat the oven to 425°F. Toss the Broccolini with 2 tablespoons olive oil and desired amount of salt, then place on a parchment paper–lined sheet pan. Bake for 15 to 20 minutes or until cooked through. Season with salt, and toss with olive oil to taste.

1. Preheat the oven to 450°F. Place the bell peppers and hot peppers on a parchment paper–lined sheet pan. Bake for 30 minutes or until tender and skins are blistered, turning the peppers over after 15 minutes. Place the peppers in a paper bag and fold it closed to let them steam so the skins loosen while they cool. When cool, peel off as much of the pepper skin as you can. Cut the peppers in half lengthwise, and remove seeds.

2. Soak the capers in enough water to cover them for 10 minutes; drain. (If your capers are brined instead of packed in salt, you can skip this step.)

3. Combine the roasted peppers, garlic, olives, and capers in the bowl of a food processor fitted with a blade attachment, and pulse until combined. Add the olive oil, and pulse to combine. Season with salt to taste.

4. Fill a large bowl with ice-cold water. Bring a pot of water to a boil, and add enough salt to make the water salty like the sea. Add the Broccolini, and return the water to a boil. Transfer the Broccolini to the bowl of ice-cold water (to stop the cooking process) using a slotted spoon; drain.

5. Spread the pepper sauce on a plate, and top with the Broccolini. Sprinkle with the nuts, if using.

MISO "CREAMED" CORN

When you think of creamed corn, you probably picture the classic steakhouse side, rich and viscous and totally unhealthy. This recipe uses a technique for making something that fills your need for a creamy dish without using any cream at all. Corn cut off the cob is gently cooked until it's lulled into a creamy state. It feels fresh yet decadent. I add miso for a hit of umami, but you can leave it out if you don't have any on hand. I recommend you use a Microplane-brand box grater for this recipe, because you need the sharpness for nicely cut kernels.

8 ears corn, shucked

¼ cup extra-virgin olive oil

2 shallots, peeled and chopped

2 tablespoons white miso (optional)

Salt

¼ cup finely chopped fresh herbs, such as chives and cilantro

Cobanero chile flakes to taste (or your favorite)

1. Grate the corn kernels from all the cobs using the large holes of a good-quality box grater set in a large bowl. You want to shred the kernels and also collect the liquid. This can be messy. Reserve 4 of the cobs for later use. (You can also cut the kernels from the cob, then use a food processor and pulse the kernels to roughly chop.)

2. Break the reserved corn cobs in half, place in a large pot, and add 4 cups water. Bring the water to a boil, turn off the heat, and let the cobs sit for at least 15 minutes to make corn broth.

3. Heat the oil in a 12-inch skillet over medium heat. Add the shallots, and sauté for 4 minutes or until just soft. Add the shredded corn kernels and any liquid from grating. Stir in 1 cup corn broth; if using the miso, whisk it into the broth before adding it to the pan. Cook, stirring occasionally, for 5 to 6 minutes or until the corn is soft and the mixture has come together. You want it to be soft, but not total mush, so some of the corn should still have some bite. If it gets too thick, you can add a little more corn broth.

4. Season with salt to taste. Transfer to a serving bowl, and top with the herbs and chile flakes to taste.

PREP TIME: 45 MINUTES   **COOK TIME:** 30 MINUTES

OVEN-ROASTED CHERRY TOMATOES AND PEAS

There's a magical time of year every summer when cherry tomatoes come into season at the same time as snap, shell, or snow peas. By oven roasting the tomatoes, you develop their tanginess and sweetness at the same time. You can use any in-season variety of peas, which are rich in fiber and vitamin C. Snap and snow peas are less starchy than shell peas. You can enjoy this as a starter over hummus, as a side dish, or as a main over pasta.

Salt

1 pint cherry tomatoes, stemmed

3 tablespoons extra-virgin olive oil, divided

1½ cups snap peas

1 cup green peas

¼ cup fresh basil leaves, chopped

2 tablespoons fresh mint leaves, chopped

1. Preheat the oven to 450°F. Bring a 4-quart pot of water to a boil and season with salt. Fill a large bowl with ice-cold water.

2. Cut the tomatoes in half and season with salt. Toss with 1 tablespoon olive oil in a bowl. Arrange the tomatoes on a sheet pan, skin sides down, and roast in the oven for 25 minutes or until they have browned a little on the bottom.

3. Meanwhile, snap off the tips of the snap peas and peel them back to remove the fibrous string on the inner edge of the pod. Blanch the snap peas in the boiling water for 2 minutes or until their color becomes brighter and they're tender but still very crisp. Transfer the peas to the bowl of ice-cold water (to stop the cooking process) using a slotted spoon, reserving the boiling water. When cool, remove the peas from the ice-cold water, dry, and cut into ¼-inch pieces.

4. Blanch the green peas in the boiling water for 1 minute or until just tender. Drain and transfer to the ice-cold water. Drain and pat dry.

5. Combine the tomatoes, snap peas, and green peas in a saucepan and cook over low heat just until warmed. Taste and season with salt as desired. Drizzle with the remaining 2 tablespoons olive oil and garnish with the basil and mint.

// THE FRUITS & VEGETABLES

PREP TIME: 20 MINUTES

TOMATO AND LABNEH SALAD

There's nothing better than an in-season tomato bursting with flavor. This salad keeps the tomatoes in their natural state and frosts them with a heaping dose of creaminess from the labneh, topped off with lots of fresh herbs. No fresh herbs? Sprinkle on za'atar spice mix instead.

4 medium-size heirloom tomatoes

Salt

½ cup labneh (store-bought or see recipe, page 28)

¼ cup olive oil

½ cup chopped herbs of your choice (basil, cilantro, parsley, mint, thyme, or oregano)

1. Core the tomatoes and cut them into wedges. Cut the wedges in half crosswise. Sprinkle generously with salt, and let stand for at least 5 minutes. Spoon the labneh onto individual plates or a serving platter. Top with the tomatoes, drizzle with the olive oil, and sprinkle with the herbs. Season with salt to taste.

ROASTED HARISSA CARROTS WITH CARROT-TOP PESTO AND AVOCADO

Carrot tops are delicious, nutritious, beautiful, and deserving of a lot better than getting plunked into your garbage can. Did you know that they have six times more vitamin C than the orange root? Perhaps Bugs Bunny should turn his around while he munches! Here, I use them to make a brightly colored green pesto. Double down with avocado, which is an excellent source of healthy fat. The whole thing gets drizzled over carrots roasted in a rich and spicy rose harissa. The result is as satisfying to the eye as to the belly.

2 bunches carrots with tops

¼ cup walnuts, toasted

1 clove garlic

¼ teaspoon salt, plus more to taste

Zest and juice of 1 lemon

¾ cup extra-virgin olive oil

¼ cup rose harissa (store-bought or see recipe, page 29)

1 avocado, peeled, cut into ½-inch pieces, and seasoned with salt

1. Pick the fine leaves off the carrot stems to equal 1½ cups. Wash and dry well.

2. Pulse the walnuts, garlic, and salt in the bowl of a food processor until combined. Add the carrot tops, and pulse to combine. Add the lemon zest and juice, and pulse again. Gradually pour the olive oil through the food chute while the processor is running, and process until combined. Season with salt to taste. Transfer the pesto to an airtight container.

3. Preheat the oven to 450°F. Line a sheet pan with parchment paper. Cut the remaining tops off the carrots, and clean the carrots (you can peel them or leave the peel on). Toss the carrots with the harissa in a large bowl until evenly coated, then transfer the carrots to the prepared sheet pan. Roast in the oven for 25 to 30 minutes or until the carrots are tender.

4. Place the carrots on a platter. Season with salt to taste. Top with the avocado, and drizzle with pesto.

PREP TIME: 15 MINUTES   **COOK TIME:** 1 HOUR

SPICY GREEN BEANS COOKED FOREVER

This recipe yields a silky, buttery, peppery bean unlike anything you've ever had before. The prep is relatively simple, but the beans need to cook for an hour or more to break down. They won't have that bright green hue of a blanched, al dente bean, but what you lose in aesthetics, you gain in texture. You will have to remind your fellow diners that there is, in fact, no butter in this recipe. Truly, you may even need a lie detector to back you up, but the vegetable itself is where the creaminess comes from.

3 pounds green beans

2 or more fresh hot red chile peppers

1 head garlic, separated into cloves and peeled

¼ cup extra-virgin olive oil, plus more for finishing

Salt

1. Trim the stem ends from the green beans. Add the beans, peppers, garlic, olive oil, and ¾ cup water to a very large, heavy-bottomed stockpot, and season with salt. Cook, covered, over low heat for 1 to 3 hours or until the green beans are just about falling apart. If while cooking you hear a lot of sizzling coming from the pot, that means that you have run out of water and will need to add a little more. When the beans are done, season them with salt and extra-virgin olive oil to taste. Serve warm or at room temperature.

PREP TIME: 15 MINUTES   **COOK TIME:** 5 MINUTES

BOILED CICORIA

According to my friend Silvestro from The Awaiting Table Cookery School in Lecce, Puglia, Italy, cicoria is the most commonly eaten vegetable in Italy. But here in the United States, it is almost completely unheard of. As its name suggests, this funny-looking bitter green is in the chicory family. In Rome, the hearts of the plants are sliced thin, soaked in water, and served with an anchovy dressing in a salad known as *puntarelle,* which is also the name of the inner stalks of *cicoria di Catalogna,* or Catalonian chicory. You can try that technique, or use this much simpler but equally delicious preparation. Can't find cicoria? You can cook other bitter greens the same simple way.

Salt

1 cicoria (or use puntarelle)

Olive oil

1. Bring a 4-quart pot of water to a boil, and season with enough salt so it's salty like the sea.

2. Meanwhile, prepare the cicoria by cutting out the heart. The very bottom of each finger-shaped spear is tough, so cut just above this area. Add the cicoria to the boiling water, and cook for 5 to 8 minutes or until softened. Drain. Serve at room temperature drizzled with olive oil.

100-LAYER EGGPLANT PARMIGIANA

Eggplant parmigiana is not something you might expect to find in a cookbook with "healthy" recipes, but it's a beloved comfort food, so I wanted a version with a major improvement over the gooey original. This eggplant is baked, the tomato sauce is simple, and it uses just a sprinkle of Parmigiano-Reggiano or pecorino cheese, and no breadcrumbs. Cooking it in a loaf pan creates a delicious showstopper. You will be surprised how many eggplants you can fit into the pan, and while I call it 100 layers, I've never been able to count how many it actually has, because people eat it too fast.

3 large eggplants (about 3 pounds), peeled

Salt

Olive oil

2 cups jarred thin cherry tomato sauce or highest-quality crushed tomatoes

1 bunch fresh basil, stemmed and chopped

1 cup freshly grated Parmigiano-Reggiano cheese or pecorino fresco

1. Cut the eggplants lengthwise into very thin slices (about ¼ inch thick or a little less). Place the slices on a paper towel–lined sheet pan or on a wire rack, and season generously with salt. Let rest for 30 minutes to extract any liquid, which will keep your final dish from being too watery. (If I'm in a rush, sometimes I skip this resting step.) Meanwhile, preheat the oven to 350°F.

2. Dry the eggplant slices with paper towels, and place them in a single layer on parchment paper–lined sheet pans. (You will need to use at least two sheet pans and cook in batches.) Brush the slices lightly with olive oil on both sides.

3. Bake for 20 minutes or until cooked through. Repeat with the remaining eggplant slices. Let cool. Increase the oven temperature to 400°F.

4. Place the tomato sauce in a bowl. Season the sauce with salt to taste.

5. Rub the bottom and sides of a loaf pan with olive oil, and line it with parchment paper. (Cut one piece of parchment paper to fit lengthwise in the pan and a second piece for crosswise

so that you have one piece for each direction of the pan. Allow an inch over the top of the pan on all sides.) Rub the inside of the parchment paper with olive oil.

6. Place enough eggplant slices on the bottom of the pan so that the entire bottom is covered. It is okay to overlap the slices, but you want to keep a relatively uniform layer. Add a thin layer of sauce, about 1 to 2 tablespoons (a little will go a long way), and sprinkle with basil and a light layer of cheese. Repeat the layers, alternating the direction you lay the eggplant with each layer and ending with cheese on top. Gently press down on the eggplant to make sure that the layers are even, and fill in any gaps. Place the loaf pan on a parchment paper–lined baking sheet.

7. Bake for 45 minutes to 1 hour or until bubbly and the top is nicely browned. Remove from the oven, and let cool for 30 minutes to 1 hour. Use the parchment paper to remove the eggplant from the loaf pan. Serve slices warm or at room temperature.

NOTE: You already know I love cherry tomatoes and making cherry tomato sauce, but you can also buy it already made. Some of the best cherry tomatoes in the world come from Sicily, and you can find sauces sourced from there at a wide variety of markets. These have just one ingredient—the tomatoes—and a complex and sweet flavor. I like the Alicos brand, as well as Agromonte. You can find both at Eataly *(eataly.com)* and other retailers. When it comes to canned whole tomatoes or crushed tomatoes, Bianco DiNapoli is my go-to brand. They have a great pure tomato flavor and the perfect level of sweetness. These organically grown tomatoes come from California, and in my opinion they are better than even the most expensive options imported from Italy.

PREP TIME: 15 MINUTES   **COOK TIME:** 45 MINUTES

ROASTED CONE-SHAPED CABBAGE

Cone-shaped cabbage (also known as conehead or Arrowhead) is an heirloom variety easy to spot at the farmers market because of its conical shape. There are several varieties, and a more common one is called Caraflex. They are available in late spring and late summer, and I find them sweeter and softer than standard grocery-store cabbages. My favorite method is to cook them on the grill or in the oven until they're caramelized on the outside and custardy in the middle. If you want a bolder flavor, top with tahini sauce before serving.

1 medium cone-shaped cabbage

Salt

Olive oil

1. Preheat a grill to medium-high heat or the oven to 450°F.

2. Remove any dirty outer leaves from the cabbage. Cut the cabbage in half lengthwise, and place on a piece of heavy-duty aluminum foil large enough to wrap the cabbage pieces. Season the cabbage with a little salt, and wrap tightly with the foil. (If your cabbage is larger, you may want to cut it into quarters.) If you're baking the cabbage, place it on a sheet pan.

3. Grill or bake the cabbage for 30 minutes. Turn the cabbage over, and cook for 15 to 20 minutes or until the core is tender. Test the cabbage to see that is it cooked and very soft by sticking a paring knife into the core. It should give easily when pierced. Transfer to a serving dish. Season with salt and olive oil to taste.

// THE FRUITS & VEGETABLES

TOMATO CHIPS

One of my favorite vendors at the Kingston Farmers Market, Long Seasons Farm, had a special price on produce if you bought an entire flat. My exuberance and frugalness led me to lug 12 pints of tiny tomatoes home. They weren't going to last long, and I had a whole lot of tomatoes and a ticking clock. So I decided to preserve them by drying them out in the oven, turning them into a tasty snack and extending their life for much longer. This is the base recipe for Tomato Powder (page 33), too.

1 pint cherry tomatoes, halved lengthwise

Kosher salt

1. Preheat the oven to its lowest temperature, around 175°F to 200°F. Arrange the tomatoes, cut sides down, on a parchment paper–lined sheet pan. Season lightly with salt.

2. Bake for 12 to 18 hours or until the tomatoes are shriveled and dehydrated. They may be a little soft when you take them out, but they will become crisp as they cool. Let the tomatoes cool completely at room temperature.

CHAPTER FIVE

THE BEANS

"LA CUCINA POVERA," OR POOR COOKING, takes us into the rich and long-established history of peasant food, translated through generations of mostly women sharing traditions practiced in the kitchens of their mothers and their mothers before them. Some of these have been lost to time as younger people opt for quicker or more elevated recipes. Yet others are so entrenched in culture, they are forever part of our shared experience. If a bowl of warm soup dotted with hearty croutons made of stale bread has ever fed your soul on a cold day, you have la cucina povera to thank.

While it's an Italian phrase, the concept of cooking with what you have access to, or what you can afford, is a wholly universal concept. And in many parts of the world that meant, and still means, beans!

THE MAGIC OF BEANS

Beans are a cheap and easy protein source with a storied past. Eight thousand years before Anthony Hopkins washed down a bowl of fava beans with Chianti in *The Silence of the Lambs* (not that I want you to channel Hannibal Lecter, but we've got favas on page 109), they were being widely cultivated along the Nile in ancient Egypt and incorporated into traditional dishes. In fact, ancient Egyptians believed favas' power went well beyond the occasional falafel and actually had supernatural powers. Considered a forbidden fruit, beans were off-limits to priests.

If it's magic beans you're looking for, the next stop is Sicily, where a drought during the Middle Ages obliterated all the crops. Villagers prayed to St. Joseph for help, and the only sprouts to be salvaged from the ground? Fava beans. If you find yourself in New Orleans, Louisiana, on March 19, you will see revelers in the streets celebrating St. Joseph's Day, beans in hand.

Now, outside the occasional *Harry Potter* film, I am no student of magic. But if there was a food upon which the masses have bestowed deep and reverent love, I'm glad it's beans. Beans are a powerful protein source. And they're so versatile in the kitchen because there are so many kinds—more than 400, actually. That number is something one of my absolute favorite bean producers, Steve Sando, owner of Rancho Gordo, found out when he started tinkering with heirloom seeds in Napa Valley, California. While his background was in retail clothing, he had become dissatisfied with the produce and beans offered at his local grocery stores. So he decided to do something about it and started growing his own. In the beginning, he applied to sell his Rancho Gordo beans at the Napa Farmers Market but was denied. He ended up at the Yountville, California, market instead, a twist of fate that would change his life.

I talked to Steve about his one-of-a-kind heirloom beans, and he was candid about those humble beginnings: "The Yountville market was really a crappy market for tourists. Lavender oil and fresh lavender were at the table right next to me. It's really hard to talk about food with this overwhelming lavender scent going on. Everyone felt sorry for me because they had sexy things like orchids and heirloom toma-

toes, and they thought, 'That poor guy's just got beans.' People would come by and say, 'I love nuts! Oh, they're beans …' and walk away."

But then one day, someone who was actually nuts for beans came by and changed Steve's life forever. That person was Thomas Keller, one of the most celebrated chefs in the world and the proprietor of two of the greatest restaurants on the planet, The French Laundry and Per Se. A seal of approval from him had the power to transform startups like Steve's from a stall in the perfumy corner of a farmers market into a thriving business. According to Steve, Keller's love of beans began with a soup his mother made throughout his childhood, and he was enthusiastic about the incredible variety of heirlooms Rancho Gordo had to offer.

Like everyone else Steve's ever told the story to, I asked what kind of beans Chef Keller bought. I waited in ridiculous, breathless anticipation for the answer.

"He liked our heirloom cranberry beans and a really obscure bean called the Vallarta from Jalisco, Mexico. It was really on the verge of extinction. But because Keller wanted it, we had to grow it, and suddenly it's thriving. It really was my lesson that the best way to save some of this stuff is to get people to eat it."

Once Steve's Rancho Gordo beans were being served at The French Laundry, other chefs followed suit. By 2018, Rancho Gordo was selling 600,000 pounds a year of 35 types of dried legumes. I discovered their beans more than a decade ago at San Francisco's Ferry Plaza Farmers Market, and they have expanded my own recipe cache.

Some people fear dried beans because they're more labor-intensive. I prefer them because dried beans are more varied, and heirloom varieties offer unique flavors, textures, and health properties. I will never tell people not to buy, use, or consume canned beans. In fact, I always have them on hand for when I don't feel like soaking and boiling and just want to get straight to the cooking. Canned beans are easily accessible and cheap, and they have shelf-life benefits that keep them always at the ready to create a healthy, longevity-giving meal. Steve agrees that it's better to eat canned beans than no beans at all. (He even kept an emergency can of garbanzos in his pantry for the first 10 years of his company.)

Rancho Gordo beans have been likened to "gems in a jewelry case," with all of their bright hues and patterns, and I don't disagree. Steve speaks of beans the way others talk about wines, describing certain varieties as having chocolate or coffee notes. But he admits others have a hard time seeing beans as a starting point. "If my idea of beans was canned red kidney beans at the salad bar, I'd hate beans, too." He tells people to start with the beans; instead of making them for a particular recipe, which can seem like a lot of work, just cook up a batch. It keeps in the refrigerator for five days, and you can build your recipes around it. Or sometimes let the beans shine on their own: "I actually think just putting the immersion blender into the beans is absolutely delicious."

I expected Steve to match my enthusiasm for beans, but what I didn't expect was what he shared next about his health. Not too long ago, he was diagnosed with type 2 diabetes. His doctor suggested he go on medication to get his blood sugar back to safe levels, which is the standard protocol. But Steve had another idea.

"I said, 'Can you please just give me three months?'" He asked for information about the types of diets and lifestyle choices that can cause diabetes to help figure out what he needed to change. "I was gonna prove to him I could do it."

He started with a very high hemoglobin A1c of 10.5 (a measure of long-term blood sugar levels). On the day we spoke—many years after his diagnosis—he had it down to 5.7 (a good value for someone without diabetes!). And he did it with—you guessed it—beans. Many people with diabetes fear beans because of the amount of carbs (approximately 45 grams per cup). But Mr. Rancho Gordo wasn't about to give them up. Steve is less interested in being svelte than he is in living a long, happy life that is filled with delicious beans and other wholesome foods. Steve also understood that the carbs in beans come with fiber. And fiber helps regulate your body's sugar levels—and keeps you fuller longer, another way to keep sugar levels in check.

It's unfortunate that despite all of the research on food and nutrition, Steve's conversation with his doctor didn't even touch on the medicinal qualities of what we grow in the ground. Too many Americans face the same issue. Thankfully for Steve, he already knew the power of beans—and how to harvest them.

FULL OF BEANS

Beans aren't just good for your health; they are good for the planet, too. Legumes are an inherently sustainable crop and boast nitrogen-fixing properties that reduce the need for fertilizers, which in turn helps decrease greenhouse gas emissions.

I use beans in a "nose to tail" practice, meaning I use all parts of the product, including the liquid they are cooked in. I know this sounds a little unorthodox, even unappetizing—that slimy water is usually just poured down the drain—but back in 2014 that cooking liquid was discovered to hold some unique properties. We now call that liquid aquafaba, and while it has almost no nutritional value, its makeup of starch and proteins makes it an interesting thickening agent or egg substitute. You'll find it enhances the sauce in my Chickpea Murphy recipe (page 107) and can be used to make an egg-free aioli (page 34).

NUTRIENT MATCHUP: CANNED VS. DRIED BEANS

Nutritionally, dried and canned beans are relatively equivalent, though canned beans have a higher sodium content, so rinse them thoroughly and look for "low sodium" on the label.

A HILL OF BEANS

It's important to note that legume naysayers, particularly in the paleo community, often point out that the phytic acid in beans bonds to the nutrients, preventing you from absorbing them. There are also countless headlines in the media about the dangers of lectins in beans and other legumes, and how they cause inflammation and digestive problems. Who knew cancel culture would come for one of the world's most nutritious foods? So let's address these claims. Phytic acid is both a healthful antioxidant and a substance that can decrease absorption of zinc and calcium. Eating a balanced diet helps you get the benefits and minimize any "antinutrient" issues. Also, the soaking process while preparing beans can decrease phytic acid levels. If you're worried about those buzzy lectins—aka proteins that plants make to help defend themselves against pests—please release this anxiety. Soaking and cooking beans destroys most of the active lectins. If this were a real issue, there wouldn't be so much science that supports beans as one of the top foods for longevity—and they wouldn't be part of *The Power Five*. Take it from someone who has worked in public health and the media to protect consumers: Be skeptical of people who create issues you've never heard of, then sell you a simple solution in a bottle to solve the problem.

LEGUMES VS. BEANS VS. PULSES

You've probably heard beans called legumes and vice versa—and never even heard of pulses. Let's break it down for you. Legumes are the family of plants that grow pods that contain seeds. Technically, when you say "legume," that includes all of the plant material—leaves, stems, and pods. "Pulses" is the name given to the edible seeds of a legume plant, which basically means beans or peas.

"CHICKENIFY" YOUR BEANS

In the beloved childhood tale "Jack and the Beanstalk," Jack is mocked for trading his cow for a handful of magic beans. Turns out, he may have the right idea. In an age where we hunger for processed, plant-based alternative meats, beans are the perfect natural alt to the alts. Beans serve as a highly nutritious and natural substitute for animal protein.

The "chickenification" of the bean is an easy strategy to make beans a main course. Nearly every go-to chicken recipe can be used for beans: bean parmesan, bean cacciatore, bean curry, even buffalo beans! Using this approach, I came up with one of my favorite recipes in this book: Chickpea Murphy (page 107).

I spent part of my childhood in New Jersey and got to appreciate the unique foods and flavors of Italian American cuisine, which were handed down through generations of Italian immigrants who created dishes inspired by their homeland. One such dish, popular in northern New Jersey, is chicken Murphy, an amusing mélange of chicken, sausage, peppers, and potatoes sautéed in a sauce made of pepper brine, white wine, chicken stock, and butter. I created a version using chickpeas instead of chicken, and let me tell you, the beans come alive. Chickpeas (also known as garbanzo beans) are my go-to bean. I know you were expecting something more exotic, but the chickpea is so easy to cook, so versatile, and—at the risk of using a cliché—it's a nutritional powerhouse. Chickpeas are rich in fiber (12.5 grams per cup) and protein (14.5 grams per cup). And studies suggest that a diet rich in chickpeas can help control blood sugar in people with diabetes, lower cholesterol, and reduce inflammation.

Now, even though chickpeas contain all of the essential amino acids, they're also low in a few of them, so they're not considered by most to be a complete protein. But if you combine chickpeas with other ingredients such as tahini or hummus (pages 113 and 196), which are made from seeds that are rich in the amino acids that beans are not, showing the wisdom of tradition, and add some whole wheat sourdough focaccia (page 136) for dipping, you are on your way to meeting your daily requirements.

BUILDING BLOCKS

When I first met Dan Buettner, I just had to ask about the relationship between rice and the people he studied in the blue zones—home to the longest-living people in the world. Rice and I have a bit of a history. When I worked at *Consumer Reports,* I ran their newly established Food Safety Center and worked on numerous stories about contaminants in the food supply. The first and biggest was about arsenic in rice. Certain types of rice contain concerning levels of arsenic, and arsenic exposure is associated with increased risk of some cancers, cardio-vascular disease, and diabetes. The work we did at *Consumer Reports* helped change policy and agriculture to make our food supply safer, though there is always more that can be done. I brought up rice with Dan because I believed it was a commonly consumed staple in some of the blue zones. He was quick to point out that people in the blue zones actually consume more beans than rice.

By example, off the coast of Okinawa Prefecture, a group of islands 400 miles south of the Japanese mainland, fish like mahi mahi are

YOUR BODY ON BEANS

When you swallow a delicious bean, its work is just getting started. As it makes its way through your digestive tract, a bean does a little dance with the friendly bacteria in your colon that ferment and convert it into a short-chain fatty acid. It's a veritable bean bacchanal! Short-chain fatty acids not only nourish your cells, but they also may be involved in sending signals to your brain. Some studies suggest beans and short-chain fatty acids make you feel fuller and could help with weight loss.

abundant, yet beans actually trump fish as the most dominant protein in the Okinawan diet. Since Okinawa, a blue zone, has a high rate of centenarians and a low rate of cancer, heart disease, and diabetes, this is more than a bit of trivia.

Okinawans consider beans to have mystical properties. But the real magic may be in the high antioxidant concentration in beans. Antioxidants neutralize free radicals (the biological scourge that damages cellular tissue all over our bodies), virtually flipping a natural off switch in our bodies. How many antioxidants do beans have, you ask? A USDA study found that red-colored beans and pinto beans ranked as high as blueberries, and black beans weren't all that far behind. One-half cup of red kidney beans has an oxygen radical absorbance capacity (ORAC) of 13,259; pinto beans, 11,864; and black beans, 4,191. These numbers represent a measure of antioxidant level. There is one big caveat to this study, though: The researchers tested the beans raw—and nobody eats raw beans. As it does for any food, cooking breaks down delicate antioxidants, so we still need to mix our beans with other colorful vegetables to maximize our antioxidant consumption.

The amino acids in beans are the building blocks of our bodies and can also be the building blocks of meals. Less than 5 percent of Americans are eating enough fiber, and that could be easily remedied by increasing bean consumption. Soluble fiber, like that found in beans, is an essential tool to naturally regulate your blood sugar and lower bad cholesterol. All in a day's work for the humble bean, ladies and gentlemen.

Now, even though I'm partial to the chickpea, beans are a fascinating ingredient that comes in all kinds of shapes, sizes, and colors. Consuming a variety of beans is important, because different strains lend unique textures and nutritional profiles to your dish, as well as varied antioxidants. There are small beans and giant beans, black beans, red beans, yellow beans, and even speckled beans. Trying some of the more colorful beans doesn't just decorate your plate; these beans also come with an extra dose of antioxidants. Much like the color in fruits and vegetables is a sign of anti-inflammatory phytonutrients, the color in beans may indicate antioxidant levels. Beans are also chock-full of potassium, vitamins, and fiber, which keeps your digestive tract moving. These little beauties may help prevent colon cancer and reduce cholesterol, so they are heart smart, too.

HOW TO SILENCE THE MUSICAL FRUIT

"Beans, beans / Good for your heart / The more you eat / The more you …" I'll let you finish one of Bart Simpson's favorite tunes, but we all know it, and for many people it's reason enough not to eat beans. Beans can increase gas because they contain sugars that your body can't break down but that gut bacteria love to feed on.

There are many culinary tricks to make beans more digestible, including cooking them with bay leaves, kombu (seaweed), fennel, or epazote. I've tried them all, and while they improve flavors, I've yet to find a study that demonstrates they can eliminate gas.

Science does support that soaking beans before cooking helps reduce gas. If you rarely eat beans, my advice is to take it slow, because the good news is, Bart is wrong. While beans can produce more gas for the bean naïf, as you make them a regular part of your diet, your body and gut bacteria adjust, returning your gut's behavior to normal.

Talking about longevity without factoring in quality of a longer life is a foolish mistake. After all, who wants to blow out 100 birthday candles if they aren't mentally and physically able to be present at the party? That's why crucial community studies, like one conducted in 2022 at the University of Tsukuba, Japan, are so enlightening. Researchers found that higher bean intake may also be associated with lower incidence of dementia. The findings are just the tip of the iceberg to uncovering the gut-brain connection that will likely dominate nutritional research for the next few decades.

Personally, I think beans are health heroes because they keep you full and are easy to work with. Here, you will find recipes that highlight beans in everything from soups to parfaits. These dishes are so good, they will make you rethink beans forever.

MORE BEANS YOU NEED TO TRY

This chapter is chock-full of beans, and there are so many varieties that you can enjoy. Here are some beautiful and delicious beans worth giving a try.

Cranberry beans, also known as borlotti beans, are an attractive pink-beige with irregular red spots. You can buy these dry (they're rarely found canned in the United States), or, when you're lucky enough, fresh at your farmers market. Cranberry beans are medium in size and creamy, and they edge out their cousin, the kidney bean, in both protein and fiber content. They're great in a salad or alone as a side with some olive oil or salt. Try them in the Beans and Greens recipe (page 110).

Black-eyed peas are eaten for good luck on New Year's Day in the South. Despite their name, they are another good-looking bean, white with a black circle. They cook quickly and have a mild flavor that I love adding to soups and salads.

Royal Corona beans, as the name implies, could be considered the king of beans. These white beans are among the largest beans I've seen, bigger than lima beans and similar in size to Greek gigante beans. They are meaty, creamy, and great in both the Beans Cooked Like Fish (page 113) and Bean Parfait (page 119) recipes.

Mayocoba beans are rich and a creamy yellow color. You can eat these whole, but I love to break them down into a luxurious mash with plenty of olive oil.

Black lentils, also called beluga or caviar lentils because of their striking resemblance to the delicacy, are among the most nutritious lentils. They are loaded with antioxidants, protein, and fiber. They typically take a little longer to cook than other lentil varieties—but they are totally worth it! Lentils are considered lucky for New Year's in Italy.

PREP TIME: 30 MINUTES, PLUS OVERNIGHT SOAKING   **COOK TIME:** 30 MINUTES

CHICKPEA MURPHY

This recipe has two inspirations. The first is the chicken Murphy at the Reservoir Restaurant in South Orange, New Jersey. It has the perfect balance of spicy and tangy, and I spent years trying to re-create the flavors in a healthier way. Then I discovered a cookbook by Joe Yonan called *Cool Beans*. Yonan's book contained the note that chickpeas are a great sub for chicken, which instantly made me conjure up this idea.

FOR THE POTATOES

2 Yukon gold potatoes

2 tablespoons extra-virgin olive oil

1 teaspoon fresh rosemary leaves, finely chopped

Kosher salt

FOR THE CHICKPEAS

5 tablespoons extra-virgin olive oil, divided

1 yellow onion, finely diced

3 cloves garlic, chopped

1 red bell pepper, cut into 1-inch chunks

½ pound shiitake mushrooms, stemmed and cut into ¼-inch-thick slices

1 teaspoon fresh rosemary leaves, finely chopped

Salt

¾ cup dry white wine

12 jarred Peppadew peppers in brine, cut in half

½ cup juice from Peppadew jar

1 (14.5-ounce) can chickpeas, drained and liquid (aquafaba) reserved

1 teaspoon chopped fresh parsley

½ lemon

1. Prepare the potatoes: Preheat the oven to 425°F. Cut the potatoes into ⅛-inch-thick slices (about 1½ cups), and toss with the olive oil, rosemary, and a sprinkling of salt. Put in a single layer on a parchment paper–lined sheet pan (or two, if necessary), and roast for 30 minutes or until crisp on the outside, flipping halfway through.

2. While the potatoes are cooking, prepare the chickpeas: Heat 3 tablespoons olive oil in a Dutch oven or sauté pan over medium-high heat. Add the onion and garlic and sauté for 7 minutes or until soft. Add the bell pepper and mushrooms, and sauté until soft and the mushrooms take on a little color. Stir in the rosemary, and season with salt.

3. Add the wine, and cook for 2 minutes or until reduced. Add the Peppadews, Peppadew juice, and chickpeas, and cook for 5 minutes. Stir in up to ½ cup aquafaba, and continue to cook for 8 to 10 minutes or until the sauce has thickened a bit and has some body. Season with salt to taste. Stir in the remaining 2 tablespoons olive oil (or to taste), transfer to a serving bowl, and top with the potatoes. Garnish with the parsley and a squeeze of lemon juice.

PREP TIME: 15 MINUTES, PLUS OVERNIGHT SOAKING   **COOK TIME:** 1 HOUR

FAVE E CICORIA

If you like hummus, you will love this classic dish from Puglia made from dried fava beans. It's topped with extra-virgin olive oil and bitter greens, which assertively cut into the warmth of the beans. You can get dried fava beans from Middle Eastern markets or online. (Bob's Red Mill sells already blanched versions that are a big time-saver, because you don't have to soak them before cooking.) I recommend using radicchio (in the chicory family), which adds a crimson kiss against the pale yellow beans, but you can sub in sautéed broccoli rabe or a green of your choice.

1 cup dried fava beans, soaked in water overnight

1 teaspoon salt, plus more to taste

1 radicchio (or other vegetable of choice)

Juice of 1 lemon

Olive oil

1. Drain and rinse the soaked beans, and add to a large, heavy stockpot with 3 cups water and the salt. Bring to a boil, skim off any foam from the top, and reduce the heat to simmer. Cook for 1 hour or until the beans easily break up. If the beans are not soft enough, add more water and cook longer as needed.

2. Use an immersion blender to blend the beans into a smooth puree. If the puree becomes too thick, add more water to loosen it up. Season with salt to taste.

3. Separate the leaves of the radicchio, and put them in a bowl of ice water to soak for at least 30 minutes (this helps reduce the bitterness). When ready to serve, drain and pat dry. Season with salt, lemon juice, and olive oil.

4. To serve, place the fava puree in a bowl. Top with desired amount of olive oil and the radicchio.

NOTE: If you use Bob's Red Mill shelled, blanched fava beans, skip soaking overnight and simply proceed with the recipe as directed.

PREP TIME: 15 MINUTES   **COOK TIME:** 40 MINUTES

BEANS AND GREENS

Beans and greens are the perfect combination for fiber and protein, and this dish has an added bonus: lycopene. Lycopene is an antioxidant in tomatoes believed to help prevent cancer. I don't usually like to cook greens to death, but Swiss chard is one that takes to being "overcooked." I like to blanch it first because chard is rich in oxalate, which can create a funny sensation in your mouth when you eat it. I find this reduces that phenomenon.

2 bunches Swiss chard

Salt

1½ cups fresh tomato sauce or crushed tomatoes (or use 1 [15-ounce] can)

½ cup dry white wine

5 cloves garlic (or use 5 cloves spring garlic)

Chile flakes (like Cobanero) to taste

1 (15-ounce) can of your favorite beans, drained (I like chickpeas in this)

Olive oil for finishing

1. Bring a large pot of water to boil. (Don't skimp on your pot size or it may boil over once you add the chard.) Clean the chard by trimming the tips off the stems and dunking the leaves in a large bowl of cold water. Repeat dunking the leaves, draining and refilling the water occasionally, until no grit remains in the bottom of the bowl.

2. When the pot of water is boiling, season with salt, and add the chard. Cook for 3 minutes. Drain in a colander. Rinse out the pot, then add the chard, tomato sauce, wine, garlic, and chile flakes. Bring to a simmer and cook for 20 minutes or until the chard is tender. Then add the beans and cook for 10 minutes or until the sauce has thickened. Season with salt to taste. Remove from the heat, drizzle with olive oil, and serve.

PREP TIME: 20 MINUTES, PLUS SOAKING OVERNIGHT   COOK TIME: 1 HOUR 30 MINUTES

BLACK BEANS AND RAMPS

Antioxidant-rich black beans are mild in flavor, have a creamy center, and could use the fragrant punch of ramps to wake them up. There are many different types of heirloom black beans, so try a new one each time you make this. The douse of citrus in this recipe, from lemon zest and lemon juice, brightens both.

2 cups dried heirloom black beans, soaked in water overnight

2 bay leaves

Salt

1 lemon

1 bunch ramps

2 tablespoons extra-virgin olive oil, plus more for finishing

1. Drain and rinse the soaked beans, and add to a medium Dutch oven with the bay leaves. Cover with cold water. Bring the beans to a boil, skim any foam from the top, and reduce the heat to simmer. Cook the beans for 1 hour 30 minutes or until tender. When the beans are done, turn down the heat to barely simmering to keep them warm, and season with salt.

2. Zest the lemon, and squeeze juice from half.

3. Clean the ramps, and separate the greens from the bulbs. Chop both finely, but keep separate. Heat the oil in a large pan over medium heat. While heating the oil, drain the beans, and discard the bay leaves.

4. When the oil is hot, sauté the ramp bulbs for 30 seconds, and then stir in the beans. Turn off the heat, and stir in the lemon zest and juice and ramp greens. Season with salt to taste, and finish with olive oil. Serve warm or at room temperature.

NOTE: If you can't find ramps, you can make this with garlic in place of ramp bulbs and use garlic chives or regular chives in place of the greens. Substitute any type of beans you want or canned black beans (if you use canned beans, skip soaking overnight, and be sure to drain and rinse the beans before adding them to the ramp mixture).

PREP TIME: 15 MINUTES   **COOK TIME:** 45 MINUTES

BEANS COOKED LIKE FISH

Chraime is a dish most sources say comes from the Jews of northern Africa. I first tasted it at Manhattan's Miznon, helmed by the famous Israeli chef Eyal Shani. This version replaces the fish with beans. It's my go-to all-seasons recipe for company. This version uses chickpeas, but I also love making it with different dried beans from Rancho Gordo, especially large white Royal Corona beans. In summer, I use fresh tomatoes and any type of spicy peppers I can find at the market.

6 cloves garlic

1 to 2 jalapeño peppers (depending on how spicy you like it and how spicy the peppers are)

¼ cup extra-virgin olive oil

1 (28-ounce) can peeled tomatoes (I like Bianco DiNapoli brand)

Salt

1 (14.5-ounce) can chickpeas, drained and rinsed

½ cup tahini

Cilantro for finishing (or use basil)

1. Preheat the oven to 425°F. Peel and crush the garlic. Cut the jalapeños into ⅛-inch-thick rounds. Heat the oil in a heavy-bottomed Dutch oven over medium heat. Add the garlic and peppers, and sauté for 5 to 8 minutes or until lightly browned. Add the tomatoes, season with desired amount of salt, and cook for 5 minutes. Stir and break the tomatoes up with your spoon. Cook for 3 minutes, and then add the chickpeas.

2. Place the Dutch oven in the oven, and bake uncovered for 30 minutes or until the sauce is thickened. Carefully remove from the oven, and put the bean mixture in a serving dish. Drizzle with the tahini, sprinkle with cilantro, and serve.

Red Lentil Soup
(page 116)

Sauerkraut, Bean, and Bread
Soup (page 117)

RED LENTIL SOUP

This is an updated version of the lentil soup recipe that appeared in *The What to Eat When Cookbook*. That soup is packed with flavor and has become a favorite, but it's labor-intensive. This version is easier to make and doesn't sacrifice any of the flavor. The caramelized vegetables and aromatics combine to create a brilliant color.

1 large leek, white and light green parts only, diced (about 1½ cups)

3 bay leaves

2 cups dried red or yellow lentils (about 14 ounces)

¼ cup extra-virgin olive oil

2 large carrots (about 8 ounces), peeled and diced (about 1⅓ cups)

1 large red bell pepper (about 8 ounces), diced (about 1¼ cups)

½ red onion, diced (about 1⅓ cups)

1 (2-inch) piece fresh ginger, peeled and finely chopped (about ¼ cup)

2 cloves garlic, minced

1 teaspoon ground coriander

1 teaspoon ground cumin

1 teaspoon smoked paprika

1 cinnamon stick

¼ cup tomato paste

Kosher salt and pepper

Rose harissa (optional; store-bought or see recipe, page 29)

1. Place the leek in a bowl of water to thoroughly rinse away any sand or dirt. Transfer to a towel to dry.

2. Bring 4 cups water to a boil with the bay leaves. Add the lentils, and cook until done, 15 to 20 minutes. Drain and remove the bay leaves.

3. Meanwhile, heat the oil in a large, heavy pot over medium-high heat. Add the carrots, bell pepper, leek, and onion, and sauté for 13 to 15 minutes or until softened and lightly browned. Add the ginger and garlic, and sauté for 2 to 3 minutes. Add the coriander, cumin, paprika, and cinnamon stick, and cook for 1 minute. Mix in the tomato paste and cook for 5 minutes, stirring often, to caramelize. Add 1¼ cups water to deglaze the pan, and simmer for 5 minutes.

4. Remove the cinnamon stick. Carefully transfer the mixture to a high-speed blender (such as a Vitamix). Let cool slightly (about 10 minutes), then puree until smooth. Season with salt and pepper to taste. You should have a bright orange puree.

5. Return the puree to the pot. Add 3 cups water, and bring to a simmer. Add the cooked lentils, and cook for 5 to 10 minutes. If the soup is too thick, add additional water; if too thin, cook a little more to thicken. Season with salt and pepper to taste.

6. Ladle the soup into individual bowls. Serve with 1 teaspoon rose harissa on top if you like.

PREP TIME: 25 MINUTES   **COOK TIME:** 1 HOUR 35 MINUTES

SAUERKRAUT, BEAN, AND BREAD SOUP

This recipe is inspired by traditions of both northern and southern Italy. In Friuli, in the north, they make a sauerkraut and bean soup flavored with pork, called *jota*. In Salento, the most southern part of Puglia, they make a cabbage, bean, and bread soup traditionally cooked in clay pots. I like to make my own sauerkraut (see page 61), but you can also buy it or use fresh cabbage instead. I make this as a spur-of-the-moment meal, so I don't have time to soak the beans. That's not a problem when using an Instant Pot. Cooking beans in a pressure cooker also helps break down the sugars that can cause gas.

1½ cups dried chickpeas, rinsed

3 bay leaves

Salt

1 pound sauerkraut (store-bought or see recipe, page 61)

2 cups leftover sourdough bread chunks (about 2 handfuls)

1 tablespoon fresh rosemary leaves, chopped

2 large cloves garlic

Olive oil

Cobanero or other chile flakes to taste

1. Place the chickpeas in the Instant Pot, and cover with 4 quarts water. Add the bay leaves, and season with desired amount of salt. Set the pot to cook under pressure for 35 minutes (if you soaked the beans, they will cook faster).

2. Put the sauerkraut in a bowl, fill with enough water to cover, and gently stir. Strain into a colander, and repeat one more time to remove extra salt. Release the pressure on the Instant Pot, and add the rinsed sauerkraut, bread, rosemary, and garlic to the cooked chickpeas in the Instant Pot, and simmer for 1 hour. Add more water, if needed, to reach desired consistency. Season with salt to taste. Ladle into bowls, and top with olive oil and chile flakes.

NOTE: Don't have an Instant Pot? No worries. You can cook this in a regular pot instead; just use canned beans.

PREP TIME: 15 MINUTES   COOK TIME: 10 MINUTES

BEAN PARFAIT

Everybody likes parfaits, so why not make one out of beans? Don't worry, it's not a dessert; it's just a bean dish with a few flavorful layers. I use za'atar, a spice mix for which the expression "If you know, you know" was born. Za'atar blends vary by region but typically contain the herb za'atar, a cousin of oregano, as well as sesame seeds and sometimes sumac. It's been used in Middle Eastern cooking for generations. It elevates almost anything you're making—from eggs to this bean parfait!

¼ cup breadcrumbs

2 tablespoons za'atar

2 tablespoons olive oil, plus more to taste

½ cup labneh (store-bought or see recipe, page 28)

2½ cups cooked white beans (if using canned, drain and rinse them)

1 cup tomato sauce (I recommend a simple cherry tomato sauce or use your own)

Salt

Chile flakes or harissa to taste

Zest of 1 lemon

1. Preheat the oven to 350°F. Combine the breadcrumbs, za'atar, and oil in a bowl, and mix. Place the mixture on a parchment paper–lined sheet pan, and bake 6 to 7 minutes or until toasted.

2. Place the labneh in a heatproof bowl that fits over a small saucepan. Combine the beans and tomato sauce in the saucepan, and cook for 5 to 6 minutes or until thickened, placing the heatproof bowl with the labneh atop the pot while the bean mixture cooks to warm the labneh. Season the bean mixture with salt and chile flakes.

3. Place the beans in a bowl, and top with the labneh, breadcrumb mixture, lemon zest, and a little more olive oil.

CHAPTER SIX

THE GRAINS

WHEN I WAS IN MEDICAL SCHOOL, I became fascinated by regional Italian cuisine. Italy is made up of 20 distinct regions where no two cooking styles are exactly alike. The fractious history has created a tapestry nation, with various dialects and cooking traditions. In fact, every town and village has their own take on traditional recipes and believes wholeheartedly that their version is vastly superior to all others. That nuance hadn't been translated to me while growing up in New York and New Jersey, where every Italian restaurant had similar offerings, all made in pretty much the same way. When I was awakened to the diversity of techniques and flavors of authentic Italian cuisine, I got swept up in cooking shows and cookbooks, even diving deep into Jewish, Middle Eastern, African, and German influences within Italian culinary traditions. That led to an earnest curiosity about regional specialties in other places, too—Hunan vs. Szechuan; Basque vs. Valencian; and so on.

During a month-long break from residency, I went to Italy on an *agriturismo* tour and to take cooking classes in Puglia. That's where I met Silvestro Silvestori. Born in America to Italian immigrants, Silvestro never felt quite at home in his native Michigan. When he was 18, he moved to Italy for good and eventually settled in Puglia, where he opened a cooking school called The Awaiting Table. When I showed up for my week-long class, the school was only three years old but already catering to tourists hungry to discover this pocket of Italian cuisine. We were all seeking authentic flavors in the southernmost part of the region, called the Salento, in a baroque town called Lecce.

Lecce is smack in the middle of beautiful but flat and dry terrain. It's a big little city at the heel of the boot, bordered by the Ionian and Adriatic Seas. As a first-time manual driver, I fumbled with the stick shift navigating the inclines in the surrounding areas quite a bit, much to the delight of the local children, who were all too happy to point and laugh at the American on holiday. In the Salento, they grow a lot of olive trees (their fruits are used to make olive oil), wild greens, and beans. They don't raise a lot of animals because of the landscape—perhaps the cows can't drive stick, either.

Luckily, Silvestro was at the wheel when he and I took a recent pilgrimage to Andria, the birthplace of *burrata,* a kind of molten mozzarella that had not yet, as of my first trip, become as ubiquitous in the United States as it is today. It truly blew my mind.

What goes better with cheese than bread? On our way back to Lecce we stopped in Altamura, where they make *pane di Altamura,* one of the best breads in the world. The bread is made with *semola* (what we call semolina in the United States), a type of flour made from durum wheat, an ancient grain that grows well in the more northern plains of Puglia. It can be difficult to work with, but durum wheat holds a lot of moisture. Known for its yellow color, it is also high in folate, protein, and iron. By law, pane di Altamura must be produced according to strict protocols, including using locally produced durum wheat and a certain specification of water. It also must use a natural leavener (sourdough starter) and have a crust that is at least three millimeters thick. I marvel at how seriously food is taken in Europe. The explicitness and adherence to old ways—the right ways—stand in stark contrast to our approach to food production in the United States. That may be how we ended up with such a broken food system, one that contributes greatly to our health problems. One thing we broke for sure is … bread.

Compared with the squishy, ultra-processed white bread that dominates grocery store shelves in America, the bread from Altamura is crusty, flavorful, and lasts a surprisingly long time on the counter. Over the past few years, I have worked in the kitchen—with the help of countless books, blogs, and calls to Italy—to create a healthy bread inspired by the one I had in Italy. The results: Pane di Staatsburg (page 138), named for my upstate New York home, which had a light coating of flour dusting every kitchen surface for quite some time due to my efforts.

BREAKING BREAD

Health professionals, like me, are always telling you to eat more whole wheat and whole grains, but we rarely offer great choices or recipes for using this member of the Power Five foods. One of the main reasons I wrote this book is to change that. I went to work in my kitchen, trying out as many types of whole wheat flours as I could, to find the best for baking, breadmaking, and pastamaking, to harness the power of the grain and give you delicious results. I discovered heirloom grain flours, like whole wheat Kamut flour, einkorn, and durum, which I recommend throughout this chapter and others.

I went in search of a utopia of better flours, and what I found was Breadtopia, a company started by a husband-and-wife team from their home base in the heart of the country's breadbasket, Fairfield, Iowa. "If you bake it … they will come" should be their tagline, because founders Eric and Denyce Rusch have developed a massive cult following of people seeking out the bouquet of flours, starters, and baking supplies they offer.

It all starts with meticulously sourced grains. Eric explained his process to me: "We're primarily looking to support a certain style of grain farming that loosely comes under the heading of 'regenerative agriculture.' We want to help create a world where the sustainable production of food goes hand in hand with regeneration of soil fertility; where each season of food production actually enhances the underground microbiome and soil structure and leaves the earth more fertile than the year before, without unnatural chemical inputs and agricultural practices that effectively strip-mine soil fertility and leave behind a dead field that requires ever-more-draconian and unsustainable inputs and practices in order to continue to produce ever-less-nutritious food."

Eric understands America's broken bread phenomenon better than most. He said, "Modern, hybrid hard red wheat (what virtually all grocery store flour is made from) is a classic case of the tail wagging the dog. The refined white flour you find on grocery store shelves has been engineered with a single goal: to last as long as possible in a bag on a shelf. Interesting flavor-producing constituents (the bran and germ) of the wheat are completely stripped out of the flour before packaging. Rather than being bred to maximize flavor or nutrition, this wheat has been bred to yield plump kernels of relatively bland and nutritionless sugar with a tiny relative percentage of germ and an often bitter but easily separated bran."

Now, looking for a whole wheat label on a loaf of bread or store-bought pasta seems easy enough, but in reality it's not. In fact, a study by researchers at Tufts University's school of nutrition found that a large proportion of people misidentify the whole-grain content of foods. The reason for that is simple: Whole-grain labels in the United States are downright confusing. So here is what you need to know when you're not baking your own: Breads labeled "whole wheat" or "whole-grain" contain whole wheat flour that has all three parts of the grain (bran, germ, endosperm), but may also be made with refined flour that contains endosperm only. Always look for breads labeled "100 percent whole wheat" or "100 percent whole-grain," because they can *only* contain whole grains and not use refined flours. Even if you buy your whole wheat bread at a bakery, it may be a mix of whole wheat and refined flours, so be sure to ask if it's 100 percent.

Luckily, consumers are beginning to figure whole grains out. I have watched with delight as healthy grain bowls and ancient flours have sprouted against the backdrop of the low-carb movement and keto-mania. It's almost like a "tale of two bowls."

I was once on a date when the server brought a basket of bread to the table and a look of fear and dread overtook my date's face.

She promptly sent the basket away, leaving me breadless instead of breathless over the prospects of romance. That date-gone-wrong illustrates how Americans have been trained to fear bread, thinking carbohydrates will ruin their diet and make them fat. Yet all over the world, grains are consumed with love and have not contributed to the kind of obesity epidemic we have in the United States. So what happened in America? How did we break bread? What led us to turn out refined, overprocessed, and sugary loaves rather than the good stuff I discovered in Italy?

There are a few answers. First, traditionally made artisan bread is fermented slowly with natural yeast and bacteria, aka sourdough starter. Time matters because the slowness of rising gives way to better flavor and texture. It also makes the bread more digestible. By comparison, commercial breads are pumped full of baker's yeast for a quicker process; they don't ferment as much as they fill up with air. Supermarket breads also often have added sugar and oil even in whole wheat loaves. Because whole wheat is harder to work with and can have more bitterness than white flour, food manufacturers often add these ingredients to improve texture and taste. But they're extraneous, and you *can* make delicious bread without them. So keep a lookout for these additives on ingredient labels.

Then there's the obvious: preservatives and dough conditioners, which aren't necessarily dangerous to us but greatly hinder the product. There's also the highly refined white flour, which is used to increase shelf life but processes out much of the fiber, nutrients, and flavor. Supermarket bread companies actually add vitamins and minerals back into the flour by "enriching" it to make it seem healthier (then they add sugar to compensate for making a poor, rather untasteful product). If that ain't broke, I don't know what is. Remember, to make great bread you only need 100 percent whole-grain flour, water, salt, and yeast.

PANE-DEMIC

I have always loved working with dough and baking my own bread. I was making pizza dough for the grill as a tween, long before it was in vogue. Not only is it one of my favorite foods, but there is something special about making it yourself. There's the aroma that fills your house and what it means to your family and friends when bread, shaped by your own hands, is served fresh out of the oven. And yet, despite my romance with breadmaking, until March 2020, I had never tackled real sourdough before.

A small but welcome positive side effect of the devastating COVID-19 pandemic was that for a brief period of time, it seemed as if everyone was making their own bread (the lesser-known *pane*-demic). It's as if learning to make sourdough bread was on everyone's to-do list and they had just been waiting for the spare time. And in the spring of 2020, most of us had *a lot* of time on our hands. I decided to join in. It was time to tend to a sourdough starter, known as a "mother." But I treated mine more like a baby in need of love, care, and feeding. I even employed my own mother to babysit during my work-from-home hours. Free daycare!

Truth be told, I was a deadbeat dad to a starter I was gifted years earlier by famed Parisian baker Eric Kayser. Like with the houseplants that came before it, I neglected that starter and have regretted it every day since. (Please read the deep shame between these lines.) But this time, suddenly everyone and their mother, literally, was baking sourdough bread. My social media feeds were filled with gorgeous home-made loaves, and I could no longer wait in the wings. I decided to give it another try and instantly became obsessed. Baking bread weekly is now a habit. I love experimenting with different recipes. And it turns out, keeping a starter going is a lot easier than I realized. (Unlike a Tamagotchi or a houseplant, a starter is actually very hard to kill.) While making the bread takes a decent amount of cumulative time, it's mostly hands-off, leaving you free to do other things. Just ask Siri or Alexa to remind you to pay attention at the right time.

I wondered if all the other pane-demic breadmakers gave up the craft when they got back to normal everyday life, so I asked Eric Rusch.

"When pandemic lockdowns prompted many who had never baked bread previously to try it, a lot of them got hooked," he told me. I wasn't sure if he caught his own dough pun, but I admired it. He went on to tell me that while sales dipped initially after the pandemic, they are now way higher than they were 2020. "There really are a lot more home bread bakers today than there were a couple years ago," Eric said. "The current trend is continued growth."

FIVE REASONS WHY I USE SOURDOUGH STARTER EVEN WHEN NOT MAKING SOURDOUGH

To start, sourdough recipes are delicious. Sourdough adds amazing depth of flavor and makes high-fiber, whole-grain baked goods better. Thanks to its high moisture content, it also has a longer counter life. Next, sourdough fermentation helps unlock nutrients, increase resistant starch, and decrease a food's glycemic index.

Keeping a sourdough starter going is pretty easy. Store it in the refrigerator and feed it a few days a week before you make bread, or keep it hungry for weeks—even let it dry out—and bring it back to life just when you need it.

And finally, it's economical. The microbes in sourdough come from the air and flour, so you don't need to buy yeast. Once you start making sourdough bread, you will have what is called spent starter, or discard, which you can use to make other things. Give it a try with my whole wheat focaccia (page 136) or my Sourdough Busiate With Trapanese-Style Pesto (page 157).

THE SCIENCE OF SOURDOUGH

Since all of the recipes in this book are *stealthily* healthy, let's talk more about how sourdough fermentation may improve the nutritional profile of bread. Sourdough recipes are fermented using wild yeast and bacteria, as opposed to the commercial yeast you buy in packets at the supermarket. These microorganisms are all around us—in the environment and on our flour. When you create a sourdough starter, you give them the opportunity to develop and grow colonies. By feeding the starter with new flour and water, you provide nutrients to help the microorganisms continue to grow and thrive.

The two prime organisms in sourdough starter are lactic acid

// THE GRAINS

bacteria and yeast. Lactic acid bacteria in a sourdough starter actually greatly outnumbers the yeast, which is surprising to some. (You can also thank lactic acid bacteria for the humble miracles that are yogurt and pickles.) These bacteria eat sugars and create acid. Yeast eats sugar and creates acid and carbon dioxide, which helps doughs rise. But it's the acid creation that gives sourdough its sour flavor. This formula—Acid + Enzymes + Bacteria + Yeast—may also be responsible for improved nutritional qualities of sourdough bread. There are other components impacted by the fermentation process, too:

STARCH: Starch is essentially a long chain of sugars. White breads are rich in easily digestible starch, which lands them relatively high on the glycemic index (the measure of how much something can increase your blood sugar levels). The process of sourdough fermentation appears to decrease the glycemic index of bread. We don't know why this is, but one hypothesis is that fermentation leads to the creation of more resistant starch that acts more like fiber than like sugar (so it doesn't increase blood sugar as much).

NUTRIENTS: Nutrients present in whole grains are impacted by phytic acid, a chemical that forms complexes with phosphorus and binds up nutrients. Gut absorption of calcium, iron, zinc, and magnesium may be blocked by phytic acid. The acid created during sourdough fermentation activates enzymes that degrade phytic acid in breads and increase the availability of minerals.

GLUTEN: The sourdough fermentation process breaks down gluten in the bread, but gluten is still present. Some people with gluten sensitivity say they can eat sourdough bread, but there are no studies to support this.

PROBIOTICS: The lactic acid bacteria in a sourdough starter are probiotics, but it's a common misconception that sourdough bread is a probiotic food. During high-temperature baking the bacteria are all killed, so none get to your gut when you eat the bread.

LET'S GET GRAINULAR

High intake of refined grains is tied to inflammation and obesity, yet eating whole grains is associated with multitudinous health benefits, including lower risks of heart disease and high blood pressure. A two-servings-per-day increase in whole-grain consumption has been associated with a 21 percent decrease in risk of type 2 diabetes, according to a meta-analysis of six large prospective cohort studies. There's also strong evidence that consuming more whole grains decreases the risk of colorectal cancer, which, according to the National Cancer Institute, has doubled in people under 50 since the 1990s. So what is a whole grain and why are all the parts important together?

A WHOLE GRAIN HAS THREE PARTS:
- The bran—a hard outer shell, where the fiber, minerals, and anti-oxidants are;
- The endosperm—a middle layer, where the carbohydrates are;
- The germ—the inside layer, where vitamins, minerals, protein, and disease-fighting plant compounds are.

Refined grains are missing one or more of these parts. White flour, for example, is made from the endosperm only. Refining grains has its advantages—it makes baking easier and more predictable, and it makes the flour last longer.

Speaking of freshness, that's another reason to get your whole wheat flours from producers like Breadtopia. Their flours are milled shortly before shipping, and the freshness of the grain means more intact nutrients and better flavor. This is important for whole-grain flours, because leaving all the parts of the grain intact means they contain more oils, which become oxidized and rancid over time.

THE "NEW" ANCIENT GRAINS ON THE BLOCK

Modern grains and flours are hybrids, grown to have certain characteristics that make them grow faster and yield larger quantities. As a result, a larger bottom line overtook quality when it came to bread. However, in health-conscious circles we have seen an increased interest in ancient grains, like freekeh and barley, and I couldn't be happier.

Now, you may be surprised not to find a single quinoa recipe in this book. Quinoa is a wonderful, healthy grain packed with protein and has become a go-to for those seeking healthier grains. The internet is chock-full of quinoa recipes, and if you are a fan, you should seek them out. But I think you've seen enough of those, and I feel there are other great options from around the world that you should try to eat in order to get more of this Power Five food. There are ironically some "new" kids on the ancient-grain block I'm excited to introduce you to. Trust me, these are heirlooms worth holding on to.

KAMUT: The wheat of the pharaohs, modern khorasan wheat is sold under the brand name Kamut. Legend has it, soon after the end of World War II, an American airman stationed in Portugal was given some strange-looking grain from a man claiming to have removed it from an Egyptian tomb. He mailed 36 kernels back home to Montana, where his father put them in the ground. I don't know if that larger-than-life story is true, but Kamut is undeniably large, three times bigger than traditional strains of wheat. It's known for its rich, nutty flavor and is one of the highest-protein grains, providing 9.8 grams per cup. It's also packed with vitamins and minerals, especially zinc,

FLOUR FRESHNESS TIPS

Smell it: Let's do a sniff test. Take a whiff of that flour in your cupboard. What does it smell like? Trick question. Fresh flour should have no odor at all. If there's a musty or sour smell, toss it. It may be rancid or its nutrients may have degraded over time.

Seal it: Flour shouldn't be stored just in the bag it comes in. You need to seal it in an airtight container or zip-top bag to extend its life.

Chill it: White flour can last one year in the refrigerator; whole-grain flour can last six months. In the cupboard, cut that shelf life in half.

carrying around 28 percent of the suggested daily value. Right now, there are only very small and limited studies on its health benefits. But early data has shown ease of digestion by IBS patients. Anecdotally, people who are nonceliac gluten intolerant have reported fewer symptoms when consuming products made with Kamut flour than white flours. That is likely due to the fact the gluten in Kamut wheat flour is biologically different from that found in modern wheats. Small studies also show that Kamut may have cholesterol-lowering properties, possibly due to its high fiber content. I like using Kamut for its nutty flavor and soft texture.

EINKORN: Meet the "mother of all grains," literally. Einkorn is believed to be the first cultivated grain variety, from which all later grains have been derived. If you're looking for a back-to-basics approach to health and nutrition, einkorn is a veritable DeLorean ride back to a time when man ate what Mother Nature handed down. It's larger than modern wheat, giving it a very different ratio of bran, germ, and endosperm, which means not only more protein but also less starch. Einkorn is genetically simple and high in protein. It also has a weaker gluten structure, which is why those with nonceliac gluten intolerance may find it easier to digest. It's rich in iron, dietary fiber, thiamine, and other B vitamins. Einkorn also contains a significant amount of the powerful antioxidant lutein. Boasting two times more vitamin A than modern wheats, einkorn may have benefits ranging from optic health to cancer prevention. I like adding einkorn flour to cakes, because even in its whole wheat form you can achieve a white flour–like texture.

DURUM: Durum wheat is lower on the glycemic scale than other grains, meaning it doesn't spike the blood sugar as much. It is often used to make pasta. Durum wheat is an iron-rich food and also contains a lot of folate. If you know someone who is pregnant, drop off a bread made with durum; they'll thank you for the folate boost! Durum wheat flour, even whole wheat, is a beautiful shade of yellow. I like adding it to baked goods when I want a little more texture in the final product.

THE FULL *MANTI*

When it comes to whole grains, we can also think beyond the bread basket. That's right, I'm talking about using our noodles, and you'll get an example of that in a Spanish-inspired recipe that uses noodles instead of rice (page 153).

Rice, forgive the pun, is a sticking point for me in the grain world. As I mentioned in our chapter on beans (page 95), in 2011 I was brought on to the *Consumer Reports* team to help with a big story on arsenic content in rice. I was in charge of risk assessment, which meant doing the analysis to figure out what the results of our study meant for human health. Arsenic, of course, is a noxious trace element that can be found naturally in the environment. But in recent years it has increased due to pollution and other factors. Arsenic can leach into plants from the soil. While a spoonful of rice won't hurt you, chronic

FIVE "NEW" ANCIENT GRAINS FOR LONGEVITY

Grain	Protein per Cup
Einkorn	36 grams
Kamut	28 grams
Durum	24 grams
Farro	24 grams
Buckwheat*	24 grams

*Despite its name, buckwheat is not related to wheat and is actually gluten free.

consumption of arsenic over a lifetime could increase risk for certain cancers and other issues. The goal of the *Consumer Reports* story was to offer recommendations for public policy to mitigate risk, rather than dropping a scary bombshell without usable takeaways. I am proud of our collaboration with the Centers for Disease Control and Prevention (CDC), Environmental Protection Agency (EPA), and Food and Drug Administration (FDA), which led to action to try to lower arsenic levels in rice. But as a cook, I was left without much love for the ubiquitous grain. It is, however, a culturally important food, and when I am dining in places where it is a vital part of the local cuisine or culture, I partake and appreciate it. However, my eyes are always open to alternatives.

When in Barcelona, Spain, for example, filled with the whimsy of Antoni Gaudí, I indulged in more than one plate of traditional paella. In Spain, you will find the dish has a crispy bottom layer, known as the *socarrat,* where rice caramelizes and toasts just a bit, adding an important textural component that's often missed in versions we find in the United States. While I indulged in rice in paella's home country, I was on the hunt for an equally delicious alternative at home. I found it in New York City's Socarrat Paella Bar, named for that crusty base. At the restaurant, they make *fideo paella,* which uses noodles instead of rice. I became obsessed with buying paella pans and creating a whole wheat version (page 153), which is also a beautiful way to sneak vegetables and beans, other Power Five foods, into meals. This chapter is full of recipes—from noodles to breads to *manti* dumplings—that will convert even the most steadfast carb-lover into a whole-grain enthusiast.

Pane di
Staatsburg
(page 138)

Ancient Grain
Whole Wheat
Sourdough
Focaccia
(page 136)

ANCIENT GRAIN WHOLE WHEAT SOURDOUGH FOCACCIA

I have been on the hunt for a whole wheat focaccia that is light and fluffy. Mission impossible—until now. For the best results, refrigerate the dough overnight to maximize flavor and texture. I am giving you two ways to make this recipe. The stretch-and-fold version helps the gluten develop and gives slightly more structure. But the no-knead variation requires less work. I like to put fresh cherry tomatoes or canned tomatoes on top before I bake. It's also great with olives hidden inside to add a healthy fat component.

140 grams starter discard (aka spent starter or leftover starter—it can be old from the fridge)

40 grams extra-virgin olive oil, plus more for finishing

10 grams table salt

1 teaspoon instant yeast

500 grams whole wheat flour (such as einkorn)

OPTIONAL

150 grams pitted black (kalamata) and or green (Castelvetrano) olives, coarsely chopped

1 pint cherry tomatoes, sliced in half (or use 1 [16-ounce] can plum tomatoes, chopped, with their juice)

Coarse salt

1. Mix 400 grams of water and the starter in a large bowl until the starter is dissolved. Add the oil, table salt, and yeast, and mix to combine. Now the messy part: Add the flour, and mix with your hands until incorporated and a cohesive, sticky dough forms. If you're using olives, add them at this time.

2. Stretch-and-Fold Method: To stretch and fold, lift one side of the dough up, stretching it slightly, and fold it over the dough toward the center, pressing the edge of the dough gently into the ball before releasing. Rotate the bowl a quarter turn, and repeat the process three more times, for a total of four stretch and folds (one entire rotation around the bowl). Let the dough rest for 30 minutes.

   Repeat the stretch-and-fold process three more times, letting the dough rest for 30 minutes between sessions, for a total of 2 hours. If you are using einkorn flour, the dough will be very sticky and the first stretch will be the hardest.

   Coat the dough lightly with olive oil, cover the bowl, and let rest at room temperature for 1 hour.

3. No-Knead Method: Coat the dough lightly with olive oil, cover the bowl, and let rest at room temperature for 3 hours or until increased in size by 25 to 30 percent.

4. Cut a piece of parchment paper slightly larger than a 13-x-9-inch baking sheet. Pour a little olive oil on the baking sheet, and spread it around using the parchment paper to help the paper stick to the pan. Transfer the dough from the bowl to the pan, and gently spread it into an even layer. Cover with plastic wrap and then a kitchen towel, and let rise for 4 to 6 hours until doubled in size. Then either bake or transfer to the refrigerator overnight and bake the next morning.

5. When ready to bake, preheat the oven to 450°F. Remove the kitchen towel and plastic wrap and, using your thumb, make light depressions in the dough every few inches. If you're using the tomatoes, spread them with their juices evenly across the top of the dough. Sprinkle with desired amount of coarse salt, and drizzle with olive oil.

6. Bake for 25 minutes or until the bread is just beginning to brown. Cool in the pan or enjoy it warm right out of the oven.

PANE DI STAATSBURG

This recipe is inspired by one of the most famous Italian regional breads, pane di Altamura. I spent more than six months trying to duplicate the reliably delicious, slightly sweet sourdough loaf from Italy—but giving it a healthier profile—and I think you will love the results. In fact, you'll rush to take a picture of this bread's thick, dark crust to share on Instagram. Don't be intimidated by the recipe's length. I want to explain the process for you in detail, because when I first started making sourdough, I needed more of a field guide than what I could find. If you're a visual learner, YouTube and my website *(thepowerfive.com)* are great places for more tips. To source sourdough starter, either reference Breadtopia's instructions on how to make your own or buy one of their starter kits *(breadtopia.com).*

150 grams fed whole wheat sourdough starter

800 grams whole wheat durum flour

200 grams whole wheat bread flour

750 grams filtered water

20 grams salt

2 (7-inch) bannetons with cloth liners (or equivalent kitchen bowls lined with kitchen towels)

1. Prepare the starter: If you keep your starter in the fridge and bake bread only once a week or every other week, start feeding your starter a day and a half before making your bread. Feed your starter about every 12 hours, so that your starter is getting its fourth feeding the morning you make the bread. Pay attention to how long it takes for your starter to double. For the first three feedings, mix 1 tablespoon of old starter with 50 grams of water and 50 grams of flour in a glass jar, so you can see it grow, and cover. (Save the discarded starter in a separate jar so you can make one of the sourdough discard recipes in this book.) For the last feeding the morning of baking, add 50 grams of water and 50 grams of flour to the jar, and mix, but set aside a small amount of the starter first, so you can preserve it. (You'll have a larger jar of discard and a smaller jar of fed starter.) Let it ferment on the countertop for several hours, but place in the refrigerator before it reaches its peak.

2. You know your starter is ready when it has at least doubled in size, occasionally bubbles, and has a dome shape. Old starter will start to collapse.

3. Prepare the bread: About an hour before your starter is ready, mix together the durum and bread flour in a large bowl, and

add the water. Using your hands, mix the flour and water together to make a dough. It will be sticky. Cover and let rest to allow the flour to hydrate—this is called the autolyse. During this time, enzymes in the flour will be activated and start cutting up the proteins to allow gluten to develop—you will be surprised how different the dough is in an hour. If you forget to make the autolyse an hour before, try to let the dough hydrate for at least 15 minutes.

4. Put 150 grams of starter onto the surface of the dough, and top with the salt. Fold the dough over from the edges to the center to cover the starter and salt. Knead the dough in the bowl for 5 minutes or until the starter and salt are all well incorporated. At first, the dough will seem to separate into thin layers; when it is well mixed, it will stop doing this and be homogeneous. Let the dough rest for 30 minutes, covered.

5. Do a series of "stretch and folds." To stretch and fold, lift one side of the dough up, stretching it slightly, and fold it over the dough toward the center, pressing the edge of the dough gently into the ball before releasing. Rotate the bowl a quarter turn, and repeat the process three more times, for a total of four stretch and folds (one entire rotation around the bowl). Repeat stretch and folds until you can't easily stretch and fold anymore—about two more times around the bowl. Let the dough rest for 30 minutes.

6. Repeat the stretch-and-fold process three more times, letting the dough rest for 30 minutes between sessions, for a total of 2 hours.

7. Let the dough rest once again for 30 to 60 minutes (or longer), until it has increased in size by 20 to 30 percent. This whole process is called the bulk ferment, because you are fermenting the dough as a whole. Next you will make the loaves.

8. Turn the dough out onto a clean work surface (you do not need to add any extra flour at this point). Cut the dough into two equal pieces, about 500 grams each, and set one aside. Cup your hands in front of one dough ball with your pinkie fingers resting atop the work surface. Slide your hands toward the dough, applying enough pressure to pull the dough ball toward you for about 1 inch, keeping the sides of your hands touching the work surface the whole time. Rotate the dough ball a quarter turn, and slide it toward you again. Do this until you have a rounded ball. This process will help to shape each dough ball into a round loaf called a boule (for beginners, there are many YouTube videos that show this process). Repeat with the second portion of dough. Cover each boule with a bowl, and let rest for about 20 minutes.

9. When you uncover your boules, they will have spread out some—this is normal. Now you are ready for the final shaping. Repeat the process you used for shaping in the previous step, shaping the loaf until you develop some tension in the dough. You can tell you are developing tension

THE GRAINS

when the dough holds its shape better and the surface looks tighter. If you develop too much tension, instead of being tight, the surface will tear or break (it's okay; just try again). Shaping takes a little practice.

10. Once you have your boules shaped, dust the tops with a little whole wheat bread flour and let rest for a few minutes on the counter so that any seams that have formed on the bottom collapse. Use a bench scraper to lift the boules off the counter and place them, upside down, into small bowls or bannetons lined with cloth or a clean kitchen towel. Place the bowls in large zip-top plastic bags, and let rest on the counter for 4 to 6 hours. Transfer the bags to the refrigerator and let rest overnight.

11. The next day, place a deep, cast-iron Dutch oven with the lid on in the oven, and preheat the oven to 500°F for about 45 minutes. Cut a piece of parchment paper to fit inside the Dutch oven, and place it on a cutting board or work surface. Remove one loaf from the refrigerator, and turn out onto the parchment paper. Using a razor or sharp knife, score the top of the loaf. I usually make a 2-inch-long "X," but feel free to score in your desired style. Using thick oven mitts (and additional mitts if needed), carefully remove the hot Dutch oven from the oven, remove the lid, and place the parchment paper and loaf in the Dutch oven. Replace the lid and put the Dutch oven back into the hot oven.

12. Bake for 30 minutes. Carefully remove the lid (then you'll get to see how much the bread rose; this is called "oven spring"). Continue to bake the bread, uncovered, for 15 to 20 minutes, depending on how dark you like the crust. Remove the Dutch oven from the oven, and put the bread on a cooling rack. Return the Dutch oven with its lid to the oven to heat for 30 minutes, and then bake the second loaf. Let the bread cool completely before slicing.

WHOLE WHEAT PANE DI STAATSBURG: Even though this is a variation, you may want to start with this version, because it's actually a little easier. Replace the durum flour with whole wheat bread flour so that you're using just whole wheat bread flour. Everything else in the recipe stays the same, except I find that this version cooks a little faster, so check it at 15 minutes after you remove the lid from the Dutch oven.

CAVATELLI (OR NOT) WITH MUSSELS AND BEANS

Cavatelli is a traditional pasta that's a tightly wrapped shell. Some describe it as looking like a hot dog bun that sauces and toppings love to hug. You may have heard that Italians never put seafood and cheese together, but there are exceptions to every rule, and this is a delicious one. Parmigiano-Reggiano thickens the sauce and adds depth to the dish. For the beans, you want to use a type with a silky texture, like cannellini, not a firm bean like a chickpea. If you want to skip the pasta, serve the mussel mixture over radicchio as a salad, or eat it on its own with a spoon.

FOR THE PASTA

1¼ cups whole wheat durum flour, plus more as needed

1 tablespoon olive oil

FOR THE SAUCE

2 pounds mussels

1 teaspoon olive oil, plus more to taste

1 stalk celery, thinly sliced

1 clove garlic, cut into thick slices

Salt

2 cups cooked beans (such as cannellini)

⅓ cup grated Parmigiano-Reggiano cheese

2 tablespoons chopped fresh Italian parsley

1. Prepare the pasta: Mound the flour on a large wooden board or work surface, and gently spread it out, making a well in the center. Pour the oil and ½ cup water into this well. Using a fork, gradually mix the flour from the sides of the well into the water. Be careful not to break the walls or the water will spill out.

2. When you've formed a ball of dough, start to knead. You will not have mixed in all the flour yet; that will happen as you knead it. Continue to work the dough, adding more flour as needed, for about 10 minutes. You are done when the dough is elastic and slightly moist but not sticky. Wrap the dough in plastic wrap, and let rest for 30 minutes.

3. Flour your work surface, pinch off a piece of the dough, and roll it out into a ½-inch-thick rope. Keep the rest of the dough covered with plastic so it doesn't dry out. Cut the rope into ½-inch-long pieces using a nonserrated knife, and roll it into a ball. Take the knife and place the flat side of the blade on the ball at a 45-degree angle. Drag the knife against the dough ball with light pressure until you've pulled it completely through the dough; the dough will curl upward as you drag. Gently remove the pasta from the knife, open it slightly, and you have a cavatelli. Place on a wire rack to dry out for

several hours. Repeat until you use up all the dough. Making pasta goes faster if you do it in a group. Don't worry, you'll get the hang of it. If the pasta is not forming because it's sticking to the table, you likely need to roll the ball in more flour.

4. Prepare the sauce: Place the mussels in a bowl, and wash several times with cold water to remove sand. Remove any visible beards. After the mussels are clean, fill the bowl with fresh cold water, and refrigerate for 30 minutes to allow the mussels to purge any sand inside. Discard any mussels that have cracked shells or are open and do not close when gently tapped. Drain just before you're ready to start cooking.

5. Heat the oil in a pan large enough to hold the mussels over medium-high heat. Add the celery and garlic, and sauté for 1 to 2 minutes or until fragrant but not burned. Add the mussels. Stir to combine and cover with a lid. Cook for 3 minutes, shaking the pan occasionally. When all the mussels have opened, drain the contents of the pan into a colander set over a bowl, saving the liquid. Discard any unopened mussels.

6. For this dish, you can keep the mussels in the shell or remove, or perhaps do half and half. If removing some or all of the mussels from the shell, do so when they are cool enough to handle, and discard the shells.

7. Bring a pot of water to a boil and add enough salt to make it salty like the sea. The pasta will cook in only a few minutes, so start it once the beans are warm in the next step.

8. Return the pan you cooked the mussels in to the stove, and add the beans and ⅓ cup reserved mussel liquid. Simmer for 3 minutes. (If you run out of liquid, add a little more. You want a saucy consistency, not a watery one.) Add the mussels, and cook until warm. Meanwhile, add the pasta to the boiling water, and cook until al dente; drain.

9. Stir the cheese into the mussel mixture; this should make the sauce thicker. Add the cooked cavatelli pasta, and stir to combine. Remove from the heat, and stir in olive oil to taste and the parsley. Season with salt to taste.

LINGUINE WITH RAMPS AND MAITAKE MUSHROOMS

Ramps are a wild onion that grow in the spring. They have a delicious, unique, pungent flavor. You often find them at your farmers market, Whole Foods, or local supermarket. Mushrooms are rich in beta-glucans, which are believed to support the immune system.

8 ounces maitake mushrooms, torn into large pieces (or use oyster mushrooms)

3 tablespoons extra-virgin olive oil, divided, plus more to taste

Salt

1 bunch ramps

7½ ounces (200 grams) whole wheat linguine (just under half of a 16-ounce package)

Cobanero chile flakes (or your favorite)

1. Preheat the oven to 450°F.

2. Toss the mushrooms with 1 tablespoon olive oil, and season with desired amount of salt. Place on a parchment paper–lined sheet pan, and roast for 30 minutes or until well browned, stirring after 20 minutes, if needed. Remove from the oven, and let rest until cool enough to handle. Then chop into rough pieces.

3. Clean the ramps by removing the roots and separating the green leaves from the stem and bulb. Wash well. Mince the roots and stems and chop the greens. Keep separate.

4. Bring a large pot of water to a boil. Add enough salt to make the water salty like the sea. Add the linguine and cook until al dente.

5. While the pasta is cooking, heat the remaining 2 tablespoons olive oil in a saucepan over medium heat. Add the ramp bulbs and stems and the chile flakes, and gently sauté for 2 to 3 minutes to just soften the ramps. Just before the pasta is ready, add the mushrooms to the ramps, and sauté for 3 seconds to warm.

6. Drain the pasta, add to the ramps mixture, and toss to combine. Turn off the heat, and add the ramp greens, mixing well until the leaves just start to wilt. Remove from the heat, and season with salt. Drizzle with olive oil to taste.

// THE GRAINS

MUSHROOM TOAST

When bread becomes toast, it undergoes a Maillard chemical reaction, which is a food-geek way to say it becomes even tastier. It also adds a crustiness, for an ever-better bed for toppings like the mushroom-tahini mixture in this recipe. This is a crowd-pleasing appetizer, but sometimes I have it for breakfast or lunch. If you're feeling fancy, garnish with thyme at the end for a picture-perfect finish.

1 pound assorted mushrooms (such as oyster, maitake, and shiitake)

½ teaspoon Urfa chile flakes (dried Turkish chile peppers)

3 tablespoons olive oil, plus more for finishing

Salt

3 cloves garlic, minced

1 shallot, finely chopped

1 teaspoon fresh thyme leaves, chopped

1 cup dry white wine

3 tablespoons tahini

4 slices whole wheat or sourdough bread, toasted and rubbed with a raw garlic clove

1. Coarsely chop the mushrooms, and add to a bowl with the chile flakes and oil. Toss to coat the mushrooms.

2. Cook the mushrooms in a large, heavy-bottomed skillet over medium-high heat for 8 to 10 minutes or until browned. Season with salt; add the garlic, shallot, and thyme; and sauté for 4 minutes or until the shallot is soft. Stir in the wine, and cook until just evaporated. Turn off the heat, and stir in the tahini. If the mixture is too dry, add 1 to 2 tablespoons water for desired consistency. Spoon the mushrooms over the toast, sprinkle with salt to taste, and serve.

BARLEY WITH HEIRLOOM TOMATOES

You can't talk about barley without talking about beta-glucan. (Well, you can, but where's the fun in that?) Beta-glucan is a soluble fiber that's been shown to significantly lower LDL cholesterol, known as "bad" cholesterol. Beta-glucans in barley are related to the kind in mushrooms but have a slightly different structure. If you are working on your numbers or trying to get off cholesterol-lowering drugs, barley can be a powerful ally on your journey. If you are someone who is genetically predisposed to have a cilantro aversion (it's a real thing!), use basil or mint. Want even more flavor? Squeeze some fresh lemon juice over the top before serving.

1 cup hulled barley

½ teaspoon kosher salt, plus more to taste

1½ cups chopped heirloom tomatoes (about 1 pound)

1 small white or red onion, minced

1 small clove garlic, minced

¼ cup extra-virgin olive oil

3 tablespoons chopped fresh basil, cilantro, or mint

1. Combine the barley, 3 cups water, and the salt in a 4-quart saucepan. Bring to a boil, reduce the heat to simmer, and cover. Cook for 20 to 30 minutes or until the barley is cooked through and softened but not mushy.

2. While the barley cooks, combine the tomatoes, onion, and garlic in a bowl. Season generously with salt to taste, and stir well.

3. Drain the barley. Add the tomato mixture to the hot barley using a slotted spoon, discarding any liquid from the tomatoes. Stir in the olive oil and basil. Serve warm.

Vegetable Manti
(page 150)

PREP TIME: 2 HOURS 30 MINUTES   **COOK TIME:** 2 HOURS

VEGETABLE MANTI

For me, wrapping dumplings is a calming act. This dumpling dish has overlapping roots in Middle Eastern, Asian, and Eastern European cultures. The dough is made with whole wheat Kamut flour, which I have found is best for making rolled egg pasta. Traditional versions use butter, but this uses olive oil for its heart-healthy monounsaturated fats and antioxidants.

FOR THE PASTA DOUGH

250 grams (1½ cups) whole wheat Kamut flour, plus more for dusting

3 large eggs

FOR THE FILLING

½ pound beets

1 bunch mustard greens, coarsely chopped

Kosher salt

¼ cup extra-virgin olive oil, divided

1 pound mushrooms, coarsely chopped (such as oyster, shiitake, or maitake)

3 cloves garlic, minced

1 small red onion, thinly sliced

TO SERVE

Salt

1½ cups tomato sauce (I like cherry tomato sauce; see page 32)

1 teaspoon smoked paprika, plus more for garnish

½ cup labneh (store-bought or see recipe, page 28)

Extra-virgin olive oil

Fresh herbs for garnish

1. Prepare the pasta dough: Put the flour on a counter or pasta board, and make a well in the center. Break the eggs into the well, and whisk the eggs using a fork, gradually incorporating the flour from the inside of the well into the eggs to make a dough. Be careful not to break the walls or the eggs will spill out. Knead the dough with your hands for 8 minutes or until it is well combined and springs back when poked with your finger. You may need to add more or less flour depending on the size of your eggs, the flour you use, and the humidity. Wrap the dough in plastic wrap, and refrigerate for at least 30 minutes or overnight.

2. Prepare the filling: Preheat the oven to 350°F. Put the beets on a parchment paper–lined sheet pan, and roast in the oven for 1 to 1½ hours or until cooked through. Let cool, and then peel and roughly chop.

3. Meanwhile, bring a large pot of salted water to a boil. Blanch the mustard greens in boiling water for 30 seconds. Drain, cool, and squeeze out excess water from the greens. Place on a kitchen towel to soak up any additional water. (You can also use an ice bath to shock the greens, if desired.)

4. Heat 2 tablespoons oil in a large sauté pan over medium-high heat. Add the mushrooms, and sauté for 6 to 7 minutes or until browned and cooked through, working in batches, if necessary, so as not to crowd the pan. Add the remaining 2 tablespoons oil between batches, if needed. Add the

garlic to the final batch of mushrooms, and sauté for 1 minute. Season with salt to taste. Transfer the mushrooms to a large bowl.

5. Add the blanched mustard greens to the pan, and sauté for 1 minute to remove any excess water from the greens. Place the greens, beets, and mushrooms in the bowl of a food processor fitted with a blade attachment, and pulse to combine. Add the onion, and pulse to combine. Season with salt to taste.

6. Prepare the dumplings: Divide the pasta dough into three equal portions. Using a pasta machine, roll one portion of dough through the 0 setting six times, dusting with flour as needed. Roll through the remaining settings two times each, adding flour between each roll and stopping at the second- or third-to-last setting on your machine. I like to make the pasta a little thicker than usual so there is less chance of it ripping once you add the filling, though you can make yours very delicate if you want to risk it. Repeat with the remaining two portions of dough.

7. Lay the pasta sheets flat on a work surface. Cut each sheet in half lengthwise (I like to fold the dough gently in half lengthwise and then open it, using the creased line in the dough as a guide for cutting). Cut crosswise into squares. Cover the dough you aren't using with a towel while you fill each square. Spoon 1 teaspoon of filling onto the center of each dough square. Bring two opposite corners together over the filling, and gently pinch the edges to seal. Bring the opposite corners over filling, and pinch the edges to make pyramids. Pinch together all the edges until fully sealed.

8. Place the dumplings on a parchment paper–lined sheet pan dusted with flour, and transfer to the freezer if not using right away.

9. To serve: Bring a large pot of water to a boil, and add enough salt to make the water salty like the sea.

10. Mix together the tomato sauce and the paprika, and heat in a small saucepan for 2 minutes or until warm. Season with salt to taste. Put the labneh in a heatproof bowl, and place it on top of the saucepan with your tomato sauce to warm the labneh.

11. Cook the dumplings in the boiling water until cooked through. When they float, they may or may not be done; the only way to tell is to feel if the seams are cooked or to taste one (but be careful; they are hot!). They should be done 2 to 3 minutes after they float. Drain.

12. Toss together the dumplings and tomato sauce in a bowl. Transfer to a serving dish, and top with warm labneh and olive oil. Sprinkle with fresh herbs or a dusting of paprika.

PREP TIME: 15 MINUTES   **COOK TIME:** 35 MINUTES

FIDEO PAELLA

This version of paella uses whole wheat pasta in lieu of rice and is inspired by a version made at New York City's Socarrat Paella Bar.

1 pound whole wheat spaghetti

6 tablespoons olive oil, divided

5 cloves garlic, minced

1 medium onion, finely chopped

1 (14.5-ounce) can chickpeas, drained and liquid reserved for Aquafaba Aioli

¼ cup diced piquillo or roasted red peppers, drained

1 tablespoon smoked paprika

Salt

1 cup dry white wine

1 tablespoon saffron threads

2 medium heirloom tomatoes, sliced or cut into wedges

Fresh basil leaves for garnish

Aquafaba Aioli (see recipe, page 34)

1. Preheat the oven to 350°F. Break the spaghetti up into pieces about 1½ inches long. Place in a large bowl, and toss with 2 tablespoons oil, then spread on a parchment paper–lined sheet pan. Bake for 10 to 12 minutes or until edges are toasted. Let cool.

2. Increase the oven temperature to 450°F. Heat the remaining ¼ cup oil in a 12- to 14-inch paella pan over medium heat. Add the garlic and onion, and sauté until softened and beginning to brown. Add the chickpeas, peppers, and paprika. Sauté for 2 minutes, then add the toasted spaghetti (fideo), and stir. Season with salt to taste.

3. Add the wine and saffron, and cook for 3 minutes or until the wine has evaporated. Stir in 3½ cups water, and bring to a boil. Cook for 5 minutes or until most of the water has evaporated, stirring occasionally to make sure the noodles cook evenly. Turn off the heat, and nestle the tomatoes in the noodle mixture. Don't overcrowd the pan; leave some room between the tomatoes so the noodles are exposed. (If you end up with too many tomato slices, make a tomato salad.) Season with a little more salt.

4. Bake for 10 to 12 minutes or until the noodles are crisp. Serve topped with basil and Aquafaba Aioli.

WHOLE WHEAT SOURDOUGH LASAGNA BREAD

Lasagna is comfort food at its best and is one of life's great pleasures. What if we applied what we love about lasagna to something else we love? Bread! Okay, I have you now. This recipe is a bit of a showboater if you want to take your sourdough making to the next level. It gets a bit messy when you are hiding thin layers of cherry tomato sauce and cheese between bread—and it's worth it.

40 grams whole wheat flour

1 tablespoon sourdough starter

50 grams extra-virgin olive oil, plus more for pan

6 grams salt

200 grams whole wheat durum flour

100 grams whole wheat bread flour

2½ cups cherry tomato sauce (see recipe, page 32, or use your own thin tomato sauce)

1 cup grated Parmigiano-Reggiano cheese

1. Prepare the dough: Combine 40 grams of water, the whole wheat flour, and the starter. Let rise until at least doubled (usually somewhere between 6 and 10 hours, depending on room temperature and your starter. I like to do this before bed, so it's ready when I wake up).

2. Combine the fed starter with 150 grams of water. Stir to combine. Add the olive oil and salt, and combine. Stir in the durum and bread flours, and mix with your hands until well combined. Let rest in a covered bowl for 30 minutes.

3. Turn the dough out onto a lightly damp work surface. Knead using the slap-and-fold technique by lifting the dough and smacking the end onto the work surface and folding the opposite side of the dough over top. Rotate the dough 90 degrees, and repeat the slapping and folding for 8 minutes (I recommend watching Breadtopia's YouTube video of this method). Return the dough to the bowl, and cover and let rest for about the same time that was required to let your starter double in size in step 1 to allow the dough to ferment (6 to 10 hours). This dough is stiff, and you may not notice it grow much.

4. Prepare the bread: Preheat the oven to 375°F. Rub a loaf pan with oil, and line it with parchment paper on all sides. (I use two pieces, one cut to fit the long way and one the short way.)

// THE GRAINS

155

5. Roll the dough to ⅛-inch thickness, aiming for a 24-inch square. (Don't worry if you end up with something irregularly shaped; you can fix it as you fold it up.) Rub the dough with olive oil, and top with a thin layer of the tomato sauce; sprinkle with cheese. Then fold the dough in half, creating a rectangle. Repeat layering with oil, sauce, and cheese, and fold in half again, so that you again have a square. Repeat layering and folding two more times, until the dough is approximately the length of the loaf pan. (It's okay if it's a little bigger.) Transfer the dough to the prepared pan (the loaf will be delicate, so use a large spatula or bench scraper). Top with a light layer of the remaining sauce and cheese.

6. Place the loaf pan on a parchment paper–lined sheet pan, and place in the oven. Bake for 1 hour, rotating the pan halfway through. If the top darkens too quickly, you can cover with foil. It's hard to tell when it's done from looking at it, so use an instant-read thermometer. It should read 212°F when inserted into the center. Let cool on a wire rack until cool enough to handle. Use the parchment paper to lift the bread out of the loaf pan or turn over to unmold. Cut into slices, and serve warm or at room temperature.

SERVES 2

PREP TIME: 15 MINUTES   **COOK TIME:** 15 MINUTES

PENNE ALLA BISANZIO

When I was a child, one of my favorite restaurants was a trattoria named Mezzaluna, where they served up a pasta dish called penne alla Bisanzio. My version captures the spirit of the original, but with whole wheat penne and sheep's milk cheese. If you avoid dairy, substitute a tablespoon of miso to add a punch of umami.

Salt

200 grams whole wheat penne

1 pint cherry tomatoes (preferably Sungold), halved

2 tablespoons extra-virgin olive oil, plus more for finishing

1 clove garlic, minced

2 ounces grated pecorino (young sheep's milk cheese)

8 basil leaves, cut into thin ribbons (chiffonades)

1. Bring 4 quarts water to a boil in a stockpot, and add enough salt to make the water salty like the sea. Cook the pasta according to the package directions until al dente.

2. Season the tomatoes with salt to taste.

3. When the pasta is almost ready, heat the oil in a small sauté pan over medium heat; add the garlic, and sauté until fragrant. Add the tomatoes and cook for 30 seconds. Drain the pasta, add it to the tomato mixture, and cook for 30 seconds. Remove from the heat, and stir in the cheese. Drizzle with olive oil, and stir in the fresh basil. Season with salt to taste, and serve.

PREP TIME: 1 HOUR 45 MINUTES   **COOK TIME:** 15 MINUTES

SOURDOUGH BUSIATE WITH TRAPANESE-STYLE PESTO

If you are making sourdough, you always have some "spent starter" sitting around, so why not turn it into a flavorful pasta? *Busiate* are a type of pasta made in Sicily, traditionally served with a tomato-basil pesto from Trapani. I learned to make this from my good friend Silvestro Silvestori, who runs The Awaiting Table, a cooking school in Puglia. Sourdough pasta needs to be cooked quickly, because if left to sit, it will continue to ferment. That's why I recommend freezing right away. If you don't have spent starter on hand, you can still make this recipe—just add an extra 125 grams of water and 125 grams of flour to step 1. I recommend using a bamboo skewer to help you shape the pasta.

1 cup (about 250 grams) spent sourdough starter

125 grams whole wheat durum flour, plus more for dusting

Salt

½ cup Trapanese-Style Pesto (see recipe, page 30)

1. Mix the starter and flour in a bowl until a dough comes together. Turn out onto a work surface, and knead for 5 minutes or until the dough feels elastic and is not sticky. You can add a little more flour if you need it, but you don't want the dough to be too dry.

2. To form the pasta, take a piece of dough about the size of a golf ball and roll it into a long rope the same thickness as a chopstick. Cut the rope into 3-inch-long pieces, and dust lightly with flour. Coil each piece around a bamboo skewer like a spring, and then roll the pasta skewer against the counter to flatten out the dough. Remove the pasta from the skewer, and place it on a sheet pan to dry. Continue with the remaining dough. Freeze until ready to use.

3. Bring a pot of water to a boil and add enough salt to make it salty like the sea. Cook the pasta in the boiling water until al dente. Drain, and toss the hot pasta with the pesto.

FREEKEH WITH BROCCOLINI AND APRICOTS

This lesser-known grain is not lesser loved by those in the know. Freekeh is easy to make, cooks up faster than other grains, and has a host of nutritional benefits. The grains are roasted, giving them a smoky, nutty flavor. Because they're a good source of the mineral manganese, they can support your immunity. This preparation is spiced with Urfa chile flakes, a Turkish chile that has subtle notes of coffee, raisins, and chocolate, to warm up the grain. Broccolini and apricot lend sweetness.

1 cup freekeh

½ teaspoon salt, plus more to taste

2 tablespoons extra-virgin olive oil, plus more to taste

½ teaspoon Urfa chile flakes (dried Turkish chile peppers)

2 bunches Broccolini, cut into 1-inch pieces

3 cloves garlic, minced

5 apricots, cut into bite-size pieces (dried or fresh, depending on the season)

1. Cook the freekeh with the salt in a saucepan according to the package directions.

2. Meanwhile, heat the oil in a sauté pan over medium-high heat. Add the chile flakes, and cook for 30 seconds. Add the Broccolini, and sauté until just tender when pierced with a fork. Add the garlic, and sauté for 1 minute. Season with salt to taste.

3. When the freekeh is cooked through, add the Broccolini mixture to the freekeh in the saucepan, and stir to combine over medium heat. Remove from the heat, and add olive oil to taste. Stir in the apricots, and adjust seasoning as necessary.

CHAPTER SEVEN

THE
FISH

I AM A BIT OF A HOME IMPROVEMENT DIYer. A few years ago, I bought a home nestled in the woods of upstate New York and have spent countless weekends renovating and tinkering to make it my dream home. If you've ever attempted a home reno project, or tuned in to HGTV, you know some walls and beams are considered "load-bearing," which means you'd better leave them alone or risk degrading the structural integrity of your house. Well, omega-3s—plentiful in fatty fish—make up the structural membranes of every cell in our bodies, and that affects their function. They also initiate the hormones that regulate blood clotting, inflammation, and the contraction of your artery walls. If Celine Dion were to dedicate a ballad to omega-3s, it would surely be "My Heart Will Go On."

I wish my reno projects gave me the kind of near-instant gratification omega-3s in fish can provide. There are actually three different types of omega-3s: ALA (alpha-linolenic acid), DHA (docosahexaenoic acid), and EPA (eicosapentaenoic acid). DHA and EPA provide the most benefits to your body—and guess what? They're both found in fish. Researchers have found that within just days of increasing daily intake of these fatty acids, there are measurable changes in cell membranes all over your body. The ones most improved are in the eyes, the brain, and the walls of the cells of your heart—the body's starting lineup! For these reasons and more, unlike most of the health promises you've heard "coming up on the eleven o'clock news," the benefits of fish consumption are *not* overstated.

The term "fat-based nutrients" (protein, iodine, and a slew of vitamins and minerals) may sound like an oxymoron, but fatty fish, such as trout, salmon, sardines, and mackerel, contain a lot of them, and they're the ones most of us don't get enough of. Fish oils are something called n-3 PUFAs (a fun-to-say acronym for the less melodious "polyunsaturated fatty acid"), and there's a large body of evidence showing consumption of this kind of fat may alleviate metabolic and cardiovascular risk. More than one large-scale, observational study has shown that people who eat fish on a regular basis have a lower risk of strokes, heart attacks, and fatal heart disease.

WHAT ABOUT MERCURY?

Great question. I was in a meeting once with a frustrated medical writer trying to make sense of mercury risks vs. health benefits in seafood, specifically for pregnant women. Medical journalists often have the herculean task of poring through data to attempt to translate findings into conversational language everyone can understand (sometimes with wonderful results, other times disastrous). This was a good (actually great) writer with a proven track record for boiling down information. But while she tried to sort through an ocean of research, she threw up her hands and asked, "Why don't they just tell pregnant women to avoid fish altogether, just to be safe?" My answer was, "Probably because of the SATs." We had a good laugh, but it's true—our brains love fish! In fact, a risk assessment done by the FDA suggested that pregnant women who ate two seafood meals a day could provide their children with a few extra IQ points (3.3, to be exact). That's because brain cells have the machinery to put omega-3s to work. The fatty acids in fish are responsible for communication between cells. In an old black-and-white movie, they would play the gum-chewing operator connecting calls.

PREVENTION ON YOUR PLATE

But let's pull back from the microscopic cellular level, where fish- and fish oil–derived omega-3s are such an MVP, to you sitting here reading this page. You may feel great today, not a pressure or pain in your body. I hope so! But it's likely you have had a bit of a headache or a muscle or joint ache that's bothered you a bit. (Let's face it, the real growing pains start at age 30.)

Often, we take aspirin to dull the pain, which works by disrupting the pathway that sends those pesky pain signals. Well, when we consume fish, the omegas do the work of shutting down inflammation pathways in a similar way—call disconnected. Inflammation is often an underlying cause when we just don't feel our best, and it has the potential to shorten our lives. So it's a no-brainer to take advantage of the power of fish to help you feel better while you live longer.

"I like big brains and I cannot lie" may never be the chorus of a hit song on the Billboard charts, but it should be. If it were, perhaps intake of fish would skyrocket. Some research shows people who eat fish regularly have larger hippocampi, one of the important memory centers in the brain. A noteworthy finding showed that people who baked or broiled their fish had more impressive brain composition than those who ate it fried. (That could be a sign of a healthier overall lifestyle, but it still impressed researchers.) Consumption of more omega-3 fatty acids, along with a diet full of fruit and limited animal meat, has also been associated with more gray matter in the brain. And seniors with high levels of omega-3s have been found to have higher cognitive function.

As our worldwide population ages and continues to live longer, finding preventive measures to ward off dementia and other neurodegenerative diseases will be front and center. I fear a growing quick-fix, brain-boosting industry is poised to meet, or exceed, the disingenuous rapid-weight-loss industry's financial hold on the population. The reality is that the benefits of fish in this area shouldn't be ignored. The science of understanding how we can improve our memory through diet is in its infancy, but there's enough evidence that shows fish could improve brain health. That sent me to the kitchen to look for new and exciting ways to prepare it.

The Mediterranean diet, which harnesses the healthiest aspects of Italian, Greek, Spanish, and other Mediterranean cuisines, has long been the gold standard for overall health. While animal proteins take a back seat to vegetables, seeds, legumes, and nuts as major components of the lifestyle, fish is encouraged twice a week. Research continues to show that the Mediterranean diet and its offshoot, the mind diet, have brain health benefits.

The Nordic diet, which mimics the eating patterns of people in Sweden, Finland, Denmark, Norway, and Iceland, is similar in principle to the Mediterranean diet and also puts an emphasis on wild seafood. When I visited Stockholm for an international meeting on food safety, I was served fish at every meal—morning to night. (Yes, breakfast too.) All Nordic countries exceed the global life expectancy again and again, and dishes that include a lot of cured fish like gravlax, salmon, and pickled herring may be why. In the United Kingdom and the United States, we fry a lot of fish, nullifying its health effects. Conversely, smoking, pickling, and preserving fish as they do in Scandinavian cooking styles help retain its nutritional benefits. Even more worrisome, while the dietary guidelines recommend eight ounces of seafood per week, most Americans are generally consuming just a fraction of that.

CHANGING TIDE: THE EVOLUTION OF AQUACULTURE

Near my home in upstate New York, a 400-mile drive from the Atlantic Ocean, there is a promised land of fresh fish. One fall day, I drove through the pine forests of the Hudson Valley and came upon a huge complex of white steel warehouses in the former industrial town of Hudson. It will remind you more of an Amazon warehouse or airline hangar than *A River Runs Through It*. Inside is a state-of-the-art, sustainable recirculating steelhead trout farm called Hudson Valley Fisheries. I was so impressed with their operation and the quality of their ingredients that I reached out to company director Paul Wong for a tour and to take a deep dive—pun intended—into the evolution of aquaculture.

It was clear right away that Paul is an inviting and cheerful man who takes sustainable farming seriously. As he talked about sustainable aquaculture, I could see a glimmer of hope in his eyes.

Overfishing has depleted our oceans of many fish. While fish is one of the Power Five foods you need to eat more of, the reality is there aren't enough fish in the sea to feed us all. Traditional ocean fishing is also very expensive, easily impacted by weather conditions and climate change, and can be unreliable. So moving to farm-raised fish seems like a natural—even ecological—solution. The problem with a lot of farmed fish is a higher risk of bacterial contamination. If you've ever kept a fish tank, you know it's very challenging to keep it clean. Now amplify that waste and debris by thousands, and you probably won't want to eat fish that's farmed the traditional way.

Fish farms are also notorious for counteracting disease among their stock with the overuse of antibiotics, contributing to the growth of antibiotic-resistant bacteria in humans. But at Hudson Valley Fisheries, they employ a recirculating aquaculture system that is a close-controlled environment. Paul calls it an "ICU," because it helps keep their steelhead trout clean and healthy. It's a large operation with a capacity of 1,000 metric tons a year (that's the equivalent of approximately 1,600 to 1,800 fish harvested every week). And it's getting pretty close to self-sustainable.

Paul told me, "We are creating a natural, cleaner environment for the fish, and as a result, we don't need antibiotics, pesticides, or chemicals. Our fish are not exposed to or impacted by the environment." That means no microplastics, mercury, or other pollutants can contaminate their fish. "The whole concept of a close-controlled environment is we have zero impact with the environment. In and out. They don't impact us; we don't impact them." Their Best Aquaculture Practices (BAP) certification means their facility proves its high standards every year.

Their facility utilizes a complicated filtration system (and is beginning to utilize reverse osmosis to reuse up to 98.9 percent of its water), upcycles its waste (fish feces are turned into organic fertilizer), and has a small carbon footprint. There's no doubt this is high-tech stuff, but Paul says you can have the best machinery in the world, and it still all comes down to the human quotient.

"There are people here who are just like the fishes' mamas. They are hand-fed a GMO-free, balanced diet of protein, natural antioxidants, and lipids at birth in the nursery tank and watched over by the dedicated experts working at the fishery. They watch how the fish act, from how fast they're swimming to how slow they're eating. It's just like raising children." They also test the water frequently, monitoring for disease. And the stakes are high. Paul told me half a million fish die if something goes wrong. I can attest that the result of all the tech and nurturing is a better fish. The steelhead trout are a beautiful shade of orange with tender, flaky lean protein.

Everyone knows about the benefits of salmon—it's one of the healthiest foods on Earth, with a megadose of heart- and brain-healthy fats. But its cousin the steelhead trout can have even more omega-3s (1.6 grams per 4-ounce serving). Steelhead trout is less fishy, with a cleaner, fresher, milder taste that even children like. It's what Hudson Valley Fisheries harvests, and their product is sought after by people who know fish best. They count five Michelin-starred restaurants, Singapore Airlines, and the iconic Manhattan bagel shop Russ and Daughters (known for their top-notch smoked fish and spreads) as customers.

FROM SEA TO TABLE

And me, of course. I have been developing recipes with their fish for years, because it's sustainable and delicious. I buy and cook Hudson Valley Fisheries fish every week, often for guests, who always remark on its freshness and flavor, while noting it doesn't overpower the dish the way other fish can.

My frequent purchases of this special fish have sent my brain racing with new ways to prepare a salmon-like fish. You'll see at least a half dozen of them in this book, including Steelhead Trout

With Rose Harissa (page 173) and multiple variations of Semi-Cured, Slow-Roasted Steelhead Trout (pages 173–175). Along with steelhead trout, I offer more ways to get your omega-3s, from salmon to shellfish, including Mussels in Saffron Sauce (page 169), Artichoke and Crab Pasta (page 185), and Roasted Oysters With Corn Butter (page 181).

PREP TIME: 50 MINUTES   **COOK TIME:** 25 MINUTES

MUSSELS IN SAFFRON SAUCE

Saffron is sexy. It has been studied for its possible libido-boosting abilities in both men and women with some positive results. But back to food: In this recipe, we create a beautiful saffron sauce for mussels, which are a great protein source for zinc and folate in addition to omega-3s. The squash adds body and creaminess without the use of cream or butter.

2 pounds mussels

3 tablespoons extra-virgin olive oil, divided

1 small onion, diced

4 cloves garlic, diced

1½ pounds yellow squash, diced

Salt

½ cup dry white wine

2 tablespoons Dijon mustard

½ teaspoon saffron threads

1. Place the mussels in a bowl, and wash several times with cold water to remove sand. Remove any visible beards. After the mussels are clean, fill the bowl with fresh cold water, and refrigerate for 30 minutes to allow the mussels to purge any sand inside. Discard any mussels that have cracked shells or are open and do not close when gently tapped.

2. Heat 2 tablespoons oil in a sauté pan over medium heat. Add the onion and garlic, and sauté until softened. Add the squash, season with salt, and cook over medium-low heat for 5 to 8 minutes or until starting to soften (don't let it brown). Add the wine, mustard, and saffron, and cook gently for 10 minutes or until the liquid has almost evaporated and the squash is completely cooked through.

3. Process the squash mixture in a high-speed blender (such as a Vitamix), gradually increasing the speed. Blend on high for 1 to 2 minutes, until the mixture is silky smooth and a vibrant yellow color. Let stand in the blender with the lid on to keep warm.

4. Drain the mussels. Heat the remaining 1 tablespoon oil in the sauté pan over medium-high heat. Add the mussels, and cook, covered, for 3 to 5 minutes, shaking the pan occasionally, until all the mussels have opened. Discard any that do not open. The mussels will give off a lot of liquid. Add ½ cup mussel liquid to the squash mixture in the blender; discard the remaining liquid. Process the squash mixture to combine, and stir into the mussels over medium heat to warm. Season with salt to taste.

Red Charmoula
Roasted Salmon
(page 172)

RED CHARMOULA ROASTED SALMON

I first had charmoula at one of my favorite restaurants in Los Angeles, Botanica, followed by one of my favorite restaurants in San Francisco, Mourad. I don't often cook recipes with so many ingredients, but I love the flavor of this mixture, and each spice adds an important element. Red charmoula is great with fish, but I also love it with roasted vegetables.

Zest and juice of 1 lemon

2 cloves garlic, finely chopped

1 teaspoon smoked paprika

1 teaspoon coriander seeds, toasted and ground

½ teaspoon cumin seeds, toasted and ground

½ teaspoon Urfa chile flakes (dried Turkish chile peppers)

2 tablespoons tomato paste

1 small plum tomato, cored and chopped

½ cup assorted fresh herb leaves, chopped (I suggest basil, shiso, parsley, cilantro, and mint)

1 tablespoon sherry vinegar

¼ cup olive oil

1½ pounds sockeye salmon (or steelhead trout)

Kosher salt

1. Add all of the ingredients except the fish and salt to a food processor, and process to combine. Season with salt to taste. Add half of the spice mixture to a zip-top plastic bag, and reserve the other half. Season the salmon with salt, and add to the bag with the spice mixture. Marinate in the refrigerator for 3 to 4 hours.

2. Preheat the oven to 400°F. Remove the salmon from the fridge and bring to room temperature. Line a baking sheet with parchment paper. Remove the salmon from the marinade, and place it on the baking sheet; discard the marinade. Top the fish with the reserved portion of spice mixture.

3. Roast until the fish's internal temperature is 120°F on an instant-read thermometer, about 15 minutes. If you like your fish cooked a little more, you can leave it in the oven for an additional 5 minutes and it will still be delicious.

STEELHEAD TROUT WITH ROSE HARISSA

A close relative of salmon is steelhead trout, which has even more healthy fats than its more famous cousin. If you're pressed for time, this is the quickest semi-cured steelhead recipe in this book.

1 pound steelhead trout

Salt

3 tablespoons rose harissa (store-bought or see recipe, page 29)

1. Preheat the oven to 350°F. Line a baking sheet with parchment paper, and place the fish on top. Season with salt, and spread the rose harissa evenly over the fish.

2. Roast until the internal temperature is 120°F on an instant-read thermometer, about 15 to 20 minutes.

SMOKED PAPRIKA SEMI-CURED SLOW-ROASTED STEELHEAD TROUT

Semi-curing with lemon and paprika overnight infuses the fish with big flavor.

1 pound steelhead trout or wild salmon

Kosher salt

1 teaspoon smoked paprika

Zest of 1 lemon

Olive oil

1. Place the fish on a piece of plastic wrap. Make sure all bones have been removed. Season the flesh side of the fish with salt. Mix together the paprika and zest, and spread on the fish. Wrap the fish tightly with plastic wrap. Put the fish on a sheet pan or in a dish, and refrigerate for 4 to 12 hours.

2. Preheat the oven to 250°F. Unwrap the fish, and place it on a parchment paper–lined sheet pan. Pour some olive oil over the fish to coat. Slow roast the fish in the oven until the internal temperature is 120°F on an instant-read thermometer, about 25 to 30 minutes.

SUMAC SEMI-CURED SLOW-ROASTED STEELHEAD TROUT 🐟

Curing is an unusual way to prepare fish, but I like it because it adds flavor and helps firm up the fish before cooking. You can cure the fish for 1 to 8 hours, depending on the thickness. The quantities of spices are a guide, so you may need more or less depending on the size of the fish and your taste. My favorite source for sumac and Urfa chile flakes is Burlap & Barrel *(burlapandbarrel.com)*.

1 pound steelhead trout or wild salmon

Kosher salt

1 teaspoon ground sumac

¼ teaspoon Urfa chile flakes (dried Turkish chile peppers)

Olive oil

1. Place the fish on a piece of plastic wrap. Make sure all bones have been removed. Season the flesh side of the fish with salt. Spread the sumac and chile flakes evenly on the fish. Wrap the fish tightly with plastic wrap; you can use the plastic to even out the spices if you need to. Put the fish on a sheet pan or in a dish, and refrigerate for 1 to 8 hours. The fish will give up a little water and help the spices stick to the fish.

2. Preheat the oven to 250°F. Unwrap the fish, and place it on a parchment paper–lined sheet pan. Pour some olive oil over the fish (use a piece of plastic wrap to rub the oil over the fish, if desired).

3. Slow roast the fish in the oven until the internal temperature is 120°F on an instant-read thermometer, about 25 to 30 minutes.

TOMATO SEMI-CURED SLOW-ROASTED STEELHEAD TROUT 🐟 🍥

I love to serve this fish on a summer day, or even a winter one, since the tomatoes are preserved. This is an excellent use of tomato powder, as the kick of umami really wakes up the mild, flaky trout. If you don't feel like making tomato powder, you can buy some from Burlap & Barrel *(burlapandbarrel.com)*.

1 pound steelhead trout or wild salmon

Kosher salt

¼ teaspoon Urfa chile flakes (dried Turkish chile peppers; optional)

¼ cup Tomato Powder (see recipe, page 33)

Olive oil

1. Place the fish on a piece of plastic wrap. Make sure all bones have been removed. Season the flesh side of the fish with salt. If you're using the Urfa chile, mix it together with the Tomato Powder. Spread the mixture evenly over the fish. Wrap the fish tightly with plastic wrap; you can use the plastic to even out the spices if you need to. Put the fish on a sheet pan or in a baking dish, and refrigerate 1 to 8 hours. The fish will give up a little water, which will help the spices stick to the fish.

2. Preheat the oven to 250°F. Unwrap the fish, and place it on a parchment paper–lined sheet pan. Pour some olive oil over the fish to coat (use a piece of plastic wrap to rub the oil over the fish, if desired).

3. Slow roast the fish in the oven until the internal temperature is 120°F on an instant-read thermometer, about 25 to 30 minutes.

PREP TIME: 30 MINUTES   **COOK TIME:** 2 HOURS 25 MINUTES

CHOUCROUTE GARNIE

Choucroute garnie is a traditional dish from the Alsace region of France, prepared with sauerkraut and preserved meats. Made simply by salting and fermenting cabbage, sauerkraut is both a prebiotic (providing fiber to feed gut bacteria) and contains probiotic bacteria when eaten raw. Smoked and cured meats, while delicious, are an anti-superfood shown in epidemiological studies to increase the risk of heart disease and death, and are considered a carcinogen by the International Agency for Research on Cancer. I've swapped the meat for seafood to double down on nutrition. You can use your favorite mix of fish and seafood, but add some salmon/steelhead to replace the traditional dish's megadose of saturated fat with heart-healthy omega-3s.

3 bay leaves

1½ teaspoons caraway seeds

1 teaspoon black peppercorns

Cheesecloth

¼ cup extra-virgin olive oil

3 carrots, peeled and julienned

2 onions, thinly sliced

4 cloves garlic, chopped

2 pounds sauerkraut (store-bought or see recipe, page 61), rinsed

2 cups dry or slightly sweet white wine (like Riesling)

8 sprigs fresh thyme, tied together with kitchen string

4 ounces smoked mussels

4 (4-ounce) fillets boneless, skinless salmon

2 (4-ounce) fillets boneless, skinless cod (or other white fish of your choice)

1 piece smoked trout

Chopped fresh parsley for garnish

1. Place the bay leaves, caraway seeds, and peppercorns in a piece of cheesecloth, and tie closed to make a bouquet garni.

2. Heat the oil in a Dutch oven over medium-high heat. Add the carrots, onions, and garlic, and sauté for 5 to 8 minutes or until softened but not browned. Stir in the sauerkraut. Add the wine and 1 cup water, and bring to a boil. Add the thyme and bouquet garni. Reduce the heat to low, and simmer with the lid on for 2 hours.

3. The sauerkraut should now be soft and even more flavorful. Stir in the mussels. Nestle all the fish fillets in the sauerkraut mixture, cover, and gently steam until fish is just cooked through and begins to easily fall apart, about 8 to 10 minutes. Garnish with parsley.

OLIVE OIL–POACHED STEELHEAD TROUT

Poaching fish in olive oil is very extravagant because of all the oil required, so this is a good dish for a weekend or special occasion. One night while I spent some time in the kitchen at David Bouley's restaurant Danube, David came in and began showing his chefs how to cook the menu perfectly. He insisted that the ingredients in the olive oil–poached fish all start at the same temperature. That's why in this recipe, I suggest you put everything together before preheating the oven. It's the Bouley way!

1½ pounds steelhead trout or wild salmon

Kosher salt

1 pint Sungold tomatoes, peeled (peeling is optional, but it is more elegant)

2 cloves garlic, thinly sliced

½ fennel bulb, cored and thinly sliced

1 lemon, thinly sliced

¼ cup kalamata or other black olives

3 sprigs fresh basil

3 cups olive oil

1. Season the fish with salt. Place all of the ingredients except the oil in a baking dish just large enough to hold the fish (an 11-x-7-inch baking dish works well here). Distribute the ingredients evenly around the fish, and then submerge them in the oil.

2. Preheat the oven to 325°F. Bake the fish until the internal temperature is 120°F to 125°F on an instant-read thermometer, about 20 to 25 minutes. Serve the fish and tomato mixture with a slotted spoon. Sprinkle with a little more salt if desired.

NOTE: To peel cherry tomatoes, bring a small pot of water to a boil. While the water is heating, score a small X in the skin of each tomato at the stem end. Fill a bowl with ice-cold water. Drop the tomatoes in the boiling water for about 30 seconds. Transfer to the water to cool. Drain and peel off the tomato skin.

TROUT "RILLETTES"

Sometimes I crave something smoky and creamy, and that can be hard to achieve without veering into an unhealthy zone. Smoked trout "rillettes" to the rescue. They're loaded with omega-3 fatty acids and lots of B vitamins. And labneh is a probiotic-rich alternative to sour cream that still delivers that craveable flavor and texture. This dip can be whipped up in a flash and is great with toasted whole wheat sourdough bread.

8 ounces smoked trout

2 tablespoons chopped shallot

1 cup labneh (store-bought or see recipe, page 28)

Zest of 1 lemon

1 tablespoon za'atar, plus more for garnish

Chopped tomatoes (optional)

1. Crumble the smoked trout into a bowl using your hands. Add the shallot, and use the back of a fork to mix together. Add the labneh, and stir with the fork until blended. Stir in the lemon zest and za'atar. Cover and refrigerate for 1 hour before serving. Top with extra za'atar for garnish (for some reason, you can never have too much za'atar) and, if desired, chopped tomatoes.

ROASTED OYSTERS
WITH CORN BUTTER

Oysters are rich in zinc, a mineral that is key for supporting the immune system. (It may also be important for supporting testosterone production.) In the public health world, oysters are a controversial food because they are usually eaten raw, which makes them a potential vehicle for the spread of infectious disease. Eating roasted oysters helps you take advantage of their nutrients without creating a significant food safety risk—and it makes them easier to open! Here, corn is transformed into a rich, buttery cream to cut the oyster's brininess in a healthier way.

1 dozen oysters

¾ cup Corn Butter (see recipe, page 35)

Sliced pickled hot peppers (or use red wine vinegar and Cobanero chile flakes)

1. Preheat a grill to medium heat. Wash the oysters to remove dirt, and discard any that are already open. Place oysters on the grill with the rounded sides down, and cover with the grill lid. (You want the round sides down because you want to try to save the liquid inside the oysters.) Cook for 5 to 6 minutes or until the oysters start to open. Most will likely open widely. For those that don't open obviously, look for the liquid inside the oysters to bubble out of the shell. This is a sign that they are cooked and will be relatively easy to open if you pay attention to the spot where the liquid is escaping.

2. Remove the cooked oysters from the grill, and carefully open them with the round sides down. Use an oyster knife or butter knife to scrape the oyster off the flatter shell. Top each shelled oyster with 1 tablespoon Corn Butter and a slice of pickled hot pepper. Carefully return to the grill, and cook for 2 to 3 minutes or until the Corn Butter is hot. Carefully transfer to a serving dish.

PREP TIME: 1 HOUR   **COOK TIME:** 30 MINUTES

SHRIMP FRIED OATS

When you think about oats, you most certainly think about oatmeal topped with brown sugar and cinnamon, or maybe even oatmeal cookies. But oats in place of rice, and with seafood? You may think I've gone too far. But try it! I've been working on creating a savory oats dish for a long time, and this one is great. While not quite a one-pot meal, it comes close! To reduce the number of dishes you dirty during prep, you can blanch the peas in the boiling water before you cook the oats.

1 cup steel-cut oats

¼ teaspoon salt, plus more to taste

¼ cup olive oil or other neutral oil (such as grapeseed), divided

2 large eggs, beaten

1 carrot, peeled and diced

1 jalapeño pepper, diced (seeded, if desired)

2 cloves garlic, minced

1 (1-inch) piece ginger, peeled and minced

2 scallions, whites and greens chopped and separated

2 pounds large uncooked shrimp, peeled and deveined

¾ cup snap peas or ½ cup snow peas, blanched and sliced into ¼-inch pieces

2 tablespoons soy sauce

½ teaspoon toasted sesame oil

¼ cup fresh cilantro leaves, chopped

1. Line a sheet pan with parchment paper. Bring 3 cups water to a boil in a saucepan; stir in the oats and salt. Cook 13 minutes or until the oats are done but still al dente. Drain and spread the oats in an even layer on the lined sheet pan. Cool in the freezer for 30 minutes to 1 hour. (You want the oats cool and dry but not frozen.)

2. Heat 2 tablespoons olive oil in a wok or sauté pan over medium heat. Add the eggs, and scramble. Season with salt to taste. Remove the eggs from the wok.

3. Add the remaining 2 tablespoons olive oil to the wok, and sauté the carrot, jalapeño, garlic, ginger, and scallion whites for 1 minute or until fragrant. Add the shrimp, and sauté for 4 minutes or until just cooked through. Stir in the peas and oats. Add the scrambled eggs, and break them up so they're well distributed.

4. Continue to sauté until the oats are hot and the shrimp turn pink, 4 to 5 minutes. Mix together the soy sauce and sesame oil, and stir into the shrimp mixture. Remove from the heat, and add the scallion greens and cilantro. Adjust seasoning, and serve.

PREP TIME: 25 MINUTES **COOK TIME:** 25 MINUTES

TAHINI-AND-TOMATO-BRAISED FISH

Falling behind on your Power Five foods? This recipe is a delicious way to incorporate a number of healthful foods all at once. It has seeds (healthy fats), vegetables (phytonutrients), and fish (it's all about the omegas, people!). Tahini is a versatile ingredient made from sesame seeds that isn't just for hummus. I mix it with tomatoes (rich in the anticancer antioxidant lycopene) to create a well-balanced and luxurious sauce.

½ cup tahini

Zest and juice of 1 lemon

1 (14-ounce) can chopped tomatoes (do not drain)

1 clove garlic, minced

¼ teaspoon ground cumin

¼ teaspoon ground coriander

Salt

1 pound white fish fillets (such as snapper, sea bass, turbot, or cod)

2 tablespoons chopped fresh parsley

1. Whisk together the tahini, lemon juice, and ½ cup water in a bowl. Stir in the tomatoes, garlic, cumin, and coriander, and season with salt to taste. Let rest to allow the flavors to meld while you preheat the oven to 375°F.

2. Season the fish with salt, and arrange it in a single layer in a baking dish just large enough to hold it. Pour the sauce over the fish (you want the fish to be swimming in it; if it isn't, reduce the size of your dish).

3. Bake until the fish is cooked through and the internal temperature is 120°F to 125°F on an instant-read thermometer, about 25 to 30 minutes. Transfer the fish and sauce to a serving platter, and garnish with parsley.

NOTE: The sauce may break in the oven. If this is the case, give the sauce a good stir before pouring it over the fish on the serving platter.

ARTICHOKE AND CRAB PASTA

This is inspired by the classic dip, usually weighed down with lots of cream cheese, on menus at many bars and restaurants. This version features the artichoke and crab in their purest and healthiest forms. I prefer to use king crab, which has a decent amount of omega-3s, but you can use blue crab, too. The artichoke base of this recipe is the *crema di carciofi* that is also in the recipe for *carciofi e pepe* pasta in *The What to Eat When Cookbook.*

1 pound king crab legs

1 (15-ounce) can quartered artichokes, drained

6 tablespoons extra-virgin olive oil, plus more to finish

Salt

400 grams whole wheat linguine, spaghetti, or home-made Sourdough Busiate (see recipe, page 157)

Pepper

1 tablespoon chopped fresh parsley

1. Cut the crab shells using a pair of kitchen shears, and remove the crab meat. Chop the crab meat into chunks and reserve.

2. Process the artichokes and oil in a Vitamix or other high-speed blender on low speed, gradually increasing the speed and pureeing until the mixture is very thick (it may not puree if you increase the speed too quickly). Scrape the sides of the blender, then shake the jar, and continue to puree on high speed, adding 2 to 3 tablespoons water, 1 tablespoon at a time, until a very smooth puree is reached. Be patient; this may take 3 to 4 minutes. Season with salt to taste.

3. Place the artichoke puree in a sauté pan with the crab meat, and warm gently over low heat while you make the pasta.

4. Bring a large pot of water to a boil. Add enough salt to make the water salty like the sea. Cook the pasta according to the package directions until al dente. Drain the pasta, reserving some of the cooking water; transfer pasta to the artichoke mixture, and stir to combine. Add a little pasta water if it's too thick. Season with pepper to taste, garnish with the parsley, and drizzle with olive oil.

NOTE: If using dried pasta, you can use the whole box if you want, but I recommend 100 grams per person.

THE FISH

CHAPTER EIGHT

THE NUTS & SEEDS

IT SEEMS EVERYONE IS SEARCHING for the next big thing in health. The truth is that sometimes the biggest impact comes in the smallest packages. Nuts are one of those tiny but mighty foods, supersized by mounting evidence showing nuts and seeds can lower your risk of heart disease and diabetes. And yet, many people avoid nuts due to their high fat content. Let me be the first to tell you that notion is outdated. Science can't point to a specific reason why, but experts believe monounsaturated and polyunsaturated fats, like the ones found in nuts, are beneficial and can lower bad cholesterol levels. Cholesterol is the pesky gunk that builds up in your arteries and makes your heart work a lot harder. If healthy fats can keep things moving cleanly, then your cardiovascular system can run more optimally for a longer time. In short, if you want to be the Betty White of your future Golden Girl clique, eat more nuts and seeds.

You will find a variety of nuts and seeds throughout *The Power Five* recipes and not just in this chapter. Nuts and seeds add texture, crunch, and a power punch of fiber and other nutrients that enhance so many dishes. I like to think of nuts as a natural substitute for fried accoutrements that come along with a lot of dishes. Think of bacon added to a plate of kale or pancetta tossed in a salad—you can achieve the same textural and flavor profiles by adding nuts or seeds instead. I also like how easily a handful of nuts and seeds can be added to anything you cook. Wouldn't it be great if every restaurant and diner had a shaker of seeds to sprinkle on your dish next to the salt and pepper? A doctor can dream, can't he?

THE NUTS AND BOLTS

Remember that old candy commercial with the catchy jingle "Sometimes you feel like a nut, sometimes you don't"? Well, those that do feel like a nut and eat them regularly may end up living longer than those firmly in the "don't" camp. Now, candy isn't the best delivery system for this health-giving food, but those who seek out nuts on a regular basis may have a sweeter life ahead of them. A Harvard study that followed more than 117,000 nurses and other health professionals for more than two decades found that those who consumed peanuts and tree nuts two or more times a week and walnuts one or more times a week had a 13 to 19 percent lower risk of total cardiovascular disease and a 15 to 23 percent lower risk of coronary heart disease. The polyunsaturated fat in nuts means they are a wonderful way to add creaminess to dishes, as every almond milk latte can attest.

One of my favorite nuts to include in recipes are walnuts. Ancient Romans feasted on walnuts, which grow all over Italy, and they considered them the food of the gods. Italian cuisine uses nuts in both sweet and savory dishes alike. The delicious California walnuts we have today are thanks to the ancient Romans who introduced them to the British who, in turn, brought them to the United States. Walnuts are full of healthy fats, fiber, and antioxidants. They also boast more omega-3s than any other nut, which is why they always show up on brain-boosting food lists. Walnuts kind of look like little brains, so maybe the gods were trying to tell us something about what they could offer us. Their ability to reduce inflammation and add non-animal protein to meals offsets their high caloric status.

Around three hours outside Florence is Italy's Le Marche region, where *girasole* (sunflowers) grow taller than the height of a basketball rim and where I attended a pop-up cooking school in a small hotel in a town called Recanati. It's there that Michelin-starred chef Franco Taruschio taught me that walnuts could be more than just crumbles on Christmas cookies and the ho-hum part of trail mix. Rather, they could be the main component in a crunchy and spicy sauce that goes great on top of butternut squash ravioli.

Back on U.S. soil, the blue zone of Loma Linda, California, offers another reason to go nutty for nuts. The researchers behind the Adventist Health Studies, which have followed the long-living members of the Adventist community for decades, found that eating nuts several times a week could cut the risk of suffering a heart attack by up to 50 percent. Most members of the Adventist community in Loma Linda follow a vegetarian diet; research on this blue zone has shown that those who eat a diet of nuts, seeds, and legumes had almost a 50 percent lower rate of premature death. It's no wonder that on his most recent visit to Loma Linda, Blue Zones founder Dan Buettner observed more than 80 bins of nuts and seeds in the Loma Linda Market. His takeaway from two decades of studying Loma Linda centenarians: snacking on nuts every day not only protects your heart but extends your life by years.

PLANTING THE SEEDS

Do you remember that movie *Honey, I Shrunk the Kids,* where Rick Moranis creates a device that zaps his kids and shrinks them to a size that's smaller than an average ant? Well, imagine when you hold a tiny seed in your hand that you are actually small enough to fit inside of it. There's a whole world within a seed to explore—literally everything needed to create complex life. There's the embryonic plant itself, and then there's a treasure trove of stored nutrients and oils that make the seed high in fiber, vitamins, and monounsaturated fats. That starter pack provided by nature is a life-giving powerhouse that we can ingest with seeds and ultimately reap the benefits of.

NUT AND SEED BUYER'S GUIDE

- Try to buy nuts and seeds in sealed packages if you can. The fat in nuts can oxidize and become rancid when exposed to air.
- Taste nuts sold in bulk or that have been around a while before you add them to a dish. They have a high probability of being spoiled.
- Store the nuts and seeds you use frequently in the refrigerator to keep them fresh and extend their shelf life. If you are using them less often (read this chapter again), store them in the freezer.
- For snacking nuts, look for raw or dry roasted. Any other type of roasting usually involves frying the nuts in oil. Go for no salt. I'm not anti-salt, but salted nuts are addictive, and tasting nuts without salt helps you learn to appreciate their natural flavors even more. You may even discover that walnuts are sweet!

Flaxseeds, like the ones in my Nut-Crusted Honeynut Squash recipe (page 197), are one of the best things you can eat to improve your digestive health. Flax is one of the world's oldest crops and its nutrition label reads like a who's who of nutritious vitamins and minerals. One of the biggest stars on the flaxseed red carpet is thiamine, a B vitamin that plays a crucial role in energy metabolism. Flaxseeds also contain copper, which aids brain development and immunity, and helps your body metabolize iron.

Sesame seeds are also health A-listers, and researchers are interested in uncovering how eating them helps our bodies, sometimes in surprising ways. A 2017 study from Brazil took a group of 20 semi-professional male soccer players and gave some of them sesame paste and others a placebo immediately before and after their training sessions. The researchers took blood panels throughout the month-long experiment. They found that the group that ate around 40 grams of sesame paste per day for 28 days had significantly reduced muscle damage and oxidative stress, as well as increased aerobic capacity.

While sesame seeds are mostly regulated to Sunday bagels and hamburger buns in the United States, in Middle Eastern cuisine they're a staple—and they should be so for us, too. I use nutrient-rich tahini, made of ground sesame seeds, as a go-to condiment or sauce for everything from fish to eggplant. It has a creamy texture and looks like a pale peanut butter, but it has a natural earthy sweetness and can even add just a hint of bitterness to a dish.

Variety is best when it comes to nuts and seeds, because each one offers your body different benefits. But they're also great eaten together. In my take on Salsa Macha (page 201), a dry salsa, you will find pumpkin seeds, sunflower kernels, sesame seeds, cashews, pecans, walnuts, and roasted peanuts all in harmony together. I like to make a bulk batch and keep it handy to sprinkle on whatever I'm eating, from toast to steelhead trout.

TAHINI

Over the past several years, I have fallen head over heels for tahini. This sesame seed paste is an easy and delicious way to get more Power Five seeds into your diet. It only takes a few minutes to turn into a sauce that goes great with just about everything.

My favorite tahinis are both made fresh by women-owned companies I order from regularly: Philadelphia-based Soom Foods *(soomfoods.com)* is a favorite of Michael Solomonov, chef-owner of Zahav. New York–based Seed + Mill *(seedandmill.com)* has a shop in Chelsea Market that also sells delicious halvah.

If you let your tahini sit for a long time, the oil and solids will start to separate. This can make it hard to use. This rarely happens to me, because of how much I use it, but when it does, I find the easiest way to homogenize the tahini is to pour the entire contents of the container into a very clean mixing bowl and spend some time whisking. Then, I pour it back into an airtight container and refrigerate.

PREP TIME: 15 MINUTES

SWEET, SPICY, AND SALTY AVOCADO TOAST

This toast is loaded with healthy fats, omega-3s, and zinc. The combination of the heat and crunch from the Salsa Macha and the sweetness of the mango with the creaminess of the avocado and salt from the salmon is awesome.

2 slices whole wheat bread (preferably sourdough), toasted and cooled

½ avocado, pitted and thinly sliced

¼ mango, thinly sliced

2 tablespoons Salsa Macha (or more to taste; see recipe, page 201)

2 pieces smoked salmon

1 tablespoon fresh cilantro leaves, chopped

1. Top the toast with the avocado, either by mashing the avocado or arranging slices atop the bread. Top with the mango, Salsa Macha, salmon, and cilantro.

PREP TIME: 1 HOUR   **COOK TIME:** 45 MINUTES

GREEN BEANS WITH WALNUT SAUCE

This recipe is really versatile. Use any green beans you have on hand or find at your local farmers market, and you'll have great results. To break with tradition and increase the power of this recipe, add ¼ cup toasted pumpkin seeds.

2 cloves garlic, unpeeled

1 cup walnut halves

Salt

1 pound green beans, trimmed (regular, French, or Romano)

⅓ cup extra-virgin olive oil, divided

½ teaspoon Cobanero chile flakes

1. Preheat the oven to 350°F. Wrap the garlic cloves still in their peels in aluminum foil, and roast for 40 minutes or until soft. Let cool, and then peel and mince.

2. Bake the walnuts on a sheet pan for 8 to 10 minutes or until fragrant and browned. Remove from the oven and cool.

3. Bring 4 quarts water to a boil, and add enough salt to make the water salty like the sea. Blanch the green beans in the boiling water for 2 to 3 minutes or until just cooked but still crisp. Drain and run under cold water to stop the cooking, or dip the beans in a cold-water bath, and drain. Dry thoroughly.

4. Place the cooled toasted walnuts in a plastic bag, and hit the bag a few times with a rolling pin or other instrument to break the nuts into a variety of smaller pieces but not into a powder. Combine the garlic and 2 tablespoons oil in a bowl, season with salt to taste, and mash with a spoon to combine. Add the walnut pieces and chile flakes, and stir to coat. Add the remaining olive oil, and let stand for 30 minutes or more, covered.

5. Toss together the green beans and walnut sauce before serving. Season with salt to taste.

NOTE: After you taste it, feel free to add a bit of acid, such as a splash of sherry vinegar, if you think it needs it.

THE NUTS & SEEDS

PREP TIME: 30 MINUTES, PLUS SOAKING OVERNIGHT   **COOK TIME:** 35 MINUTES

SMOKY EGGPLANT WITH HUMMUS

In Middle Eastern cooking, hummus is often served warm with meat toppings. This preparation substitutes smoky eggplant—grilled whole here—for the traditional beef or lamb. If you substitute canned chickpeas for dried, just heat them before making the hummus. Use most of the olive oil as a finisher to add a peppery richness and preserve the healthy antioxidants that olive oil brings. Choose "first pressed" oil if you can, and opt for one that has a green hue and tickles your throat a bit.

FOR THE HUMMUS

1 cup dried chickpeas

1 teaspoon salt, plus more to taste

4 cloves garlic

Juice of 2 lemons

¾ cup tahini

½ teaspoon ground cumin, plus more to taste

1 teaspoon baking soda

FOR THE EGGPLANT

1 large or 2 small eggplants

1 tablespoon olive oil

2 cloves garlic, chopped

½ teaspoon smoked paprika

FOR SERVING

Extra-virgin olive oil

1 tablespoon chopped fresh parsley or cilantro

Crunchy bread or warmed whole wheat pita

1. Prepare the hummus: Soak the chickpeas overnight in 4 quarts water and the salt.

2. The next day, process the garlic in a food processor. Add the lemon juice, and pulse to combine. Let sit for 15 minutes. Add the tahini, and pulse to combine. The tahini sauce will likely become very thick. Add enough cold water gradually while processing until the sauce reaches the consistency of yogurt, adding no more than ½ cup water. Add the cumin, and season with salt to taste.

3. Drain the chickpeas, place in a Dutch oven, and cover with cold water. Add the baking soda (to help soften the chickpeas), and bring to a simmer. Skim the foam from the top of the beans, and reduce the heat to maintain a low simmer. Cook for 30 to 45 minutes or until the beans are soft.

4. Meanwhile, prepare the eggplant: Preheat a grill to medium-high heat. Add the eggplant, and grill, covered with the grill lid and turning occasionally, 15 to 20 minutes or until the skin is charred and the eggplant is tender. (You can also bake the eggplant at 500°F on a sheet pan for 20 to 25 minutes for a large eggplant, turning halfway through.) Remove the skin and chop the flesh.

5. Heat the oil in a saucepan over medium heat. Add the garlic, and sauté for 1 minute. Stir in the paprika until blended; stir in the eggplant. Cook for 3 minutes, season with salt to taste, and keep warm.

6. Drain the chickpeas, and add to the tahini sauce in the food processor. Process until smooth. Season with salt and additional cumin to taste.

7. To serve, transfer the warm hummus to a dish (if the hummus has cooled, you can warm it in a double boiler) and make a well in the center. Fill the well with the eggplant, and top with extra-virgin olive oil. Garnish with the herbs, and serve with crunchy bread or pita.

SERVES 4 TO 6

PREP TIME: 15 MINUTES   **COOK TIME:** 40 MINUTES

NUT-CRUSTED HONEYNUT SQUASH

When heat meets sweet, very little can go wrong, flavorwise. In making this, you layer flavors: the sweetness of honeynut squash, the spice of harissa, and the toasty, creamy crunch of the protein-rich, healthy-fat nut-butter crust. Butternut squash has had a renaissance in the past few years, and honeynut is its smaller, sweeter cousin with edible skin (so you don't have to peel it). Try swapping chile crisp—a spicy, fragrant condiment—for the harissa to make a dish with a more Asian flavor profile.

½ cup Mixed Nut Butter (see recipe, page 35)

1 tablespoon rose harissa (store-bought or see recipe, page 29)

Salt

2 honeynut squash or 1 small butternut squash

Olive oil

Chopped fresh herbs (cilantro, basil, parsley, or chives)

1. Preheat the oven to 375°F. Combine the nut butter and harissa, adding more or less of each depending on your preference. Season with salt to taste.

2. Cut the squash in half, and remove the seeds. Coat lightly with olive oil, and sprinkle with the nut butter mixture, coating evenly. Place on a parchment paper–lined sheet pan.

3. Roast in the oven for 40 to 45 minutes or until the squash is cooked through and a paring knife inserted into the flesh comes out clean. Top with the chopped herbs, drizzle with a little olive oil, and serve.

Spicy Cucumber
Salad (page 200)

Salsa Macha
(page 201)

SPICY CUCUMBER SALAD

I love cucumber salads. This water-rich vegetable makes a great guilt-free snack because of its crunch. It's also a refreshing side. Much of a cucumber's nutrition is in its skin, so I leave it on here.

6 Persian cucumbers, cut into ½-inch half-moon slices

Salt

¼ cup Salsa Macha (see recipe, opposite)

1 tablespoon sherry vinegar (or other acid)

2 tablespoons chopped fresh cilantro, mint, or basil

1. Season the cucumbers with salt in a bowl, and let stand for 1 hour. Drain off water, and then mix in the Salsa Macha and vinegar. Let stand at room temperature for at least 1 hour. Stir in the herbs. Serve immediately, or refrigerate overnight to marinate further.

SALSA MACHA

Sometimes called a dry salsa, this condiment originates in the Veracruz region of Mexico. This version is loaded with some of the most undereaten ingredients (nuts and seeds). It's chock-full of protein, healthy fat, and zinc, a harder-to-get mineral important both for immunity and regulating sex hormones (like testosterone). I like it spicy; adjust the heat by using only one type of chile or adding more nuts and seeds. Try it on anything from green beans and chicken to soups and stews.

¼ cup raw cashews

¼ cup raw pecans

¼ cup raw walnuts

½ cup extra-virgin olive oil, divided

1 dried chipotle chile pepper

5 cloves garlic, minced

¼ teaspoon Cobanero chile flakes

¼ cup pumpkin seeds

¼ cup sunflower kernels

2 tablespoons sesame seeds

¼ cup roasted unsalted peanuts

Salt

1. Preheat the oven to 350°F. Roast the cashews, pecans, and walnuts in a single layer on a baking sheet for 8 minutes. Remove from the oven and cool.

2. Heat ¼ cup oil in a small sauté pan, and cook the chile pepper over medium-low heat for 1 minute on each side. It will become fragrant. Remove from the pan and cool.

3. Add the garlic to the hot oil, and cook gently until just browning (you may need to reduce the heat). Stir in the chile flakes until blended, then stir in the pumpkin seeds, sunflower kernels, and sesame seeds. Cook for 2 minutes. Remove from the heat and cool.

4. Process the cooled chile pepper in a food processor until broken into very small pieces. Add all the toasted nuts, the peanuts, and the seed-garlic mixture. Season with salt to taste. Pulse several times until the nuts are broken into smaller pieces, but not so many times that it becomes a fine mince or a paste—you want it to have a good texture.

5. Transfer the mixture to an airtight container, and stir in the remaining ¼ cup oil (add more if you need it). Serve immediately, or cover and chill up to 10 days. If you refrigerate it, let it stand at room temperature to let oil return to a liquid state before serving.

PREP TIME: 5 MINUTES   **COOK TIME:** 30 MINUTES

GRILLED EGGPLANT

This is a simple, delicious way to enjoy eggplant without having to fry it or add a ton of cheese. If yours starts to fall apart, remove all the flesh from the skin and place it in a bowl to serve. Look for eggplant that has a sheen to its skin; it should be firm but not hard. If you push in with your finger and puncture the skin, it's overripe.

1 large eggplant

Salt

TOPPINGS

Olive oil

Tahini or tahini sauce

Chopped jalapeño peppers

Chopped assorted fresh herbs
(such as basil, mint, and parsley)

1. Preheat a grill to medium-high heat. Add the eggplant, and grill, covered with the grill lid and turning occasionally, for 30 minutes or until charred on all sides and the eggplant is just about to fall apart. Transfer to a serving dish, and slice open down the middle. Season with salt, sprinkle with desired toppings, and serve.

ROASTED LION'S MANE MUSHROOMS WITH WHIPPED TAHINI

Lion's mane mushrooms have a long history of use in Asia for both culinary and medicinal purposes. They're very "meaty" and remind me of sweetbreads. Whipped Tahini (see page 34) is a vegan cream sauce made from pureed sesame seeds. It's a lovely way to add richness to mushrooms or virtually anything that could be made a little richer—and more delicious—with a little cream. Add garlic to it for a pungent note.

½ pound lion's mane mushrooms

2 to 4 tablespoons rose harissa (store-bought or see recipe, page 29)

¼ cup Whipped Tahini (see recipe, page 34)

Extra-virgin olive oil (optional)

Cobanero chile flakes (optional)

1. Preheat the oven to 425°F. Line a sheet pan with parchment paper. Coat the tops of the mushrooms with the rose harissa, and place on the sheet pan. Roast for 45 minutes or until the harissa is a dark red and the mushrooms are tender when poked with a skewer or paring knife. (If your mushrooms are small, they may cook faster.) You may need to turn the pan and mushrooms occasionally so they cook evenly.

2. Spread the tahini on a plate. Cut the mushrooms into ¼-inch-thick slices, and serve with the tahini. If desired, drizzle the tahini with oil and sprinkle with chile flakes.

PART THREE

EAT LESS

Now it's time to get into the foods that you should eat less of: meats and sweets. These are the foods I call the "undeniables," because to deny yourself of them completely is not a sustainable approach to Power Five eating. I want you to have recipes that are made of whole, nutritious ingredients. Here's the bonus: I won't tell you anything is "guilt free," because food should *always* be free of judgment and bring you joy.

CHAPTER NINE

THE MEATS

THE FIRST "UNDENIABLE" FOOD (if you aren't a vegan or vege-tarian) is meat. Let's cut to the chase: In a study out of the Harvard T.H. Chan School of Public Health, Dr. Walter Willett and his fellow researchers followed 100,000 people for two decades and found that higher consumption of red meat was linked to an increased risk of premature death. When looking at those who consumed one serving of meat a day, or less, the risk was significantly lower. In the same study, poultry was shown to be less risky than red meat. (In fact, chicken is included in this chapter because it is a meat, but over and over again, science shows us this lean protein comes with significantly less risk than red or processed meats.) The Har-vard study doesn't exist alone on an island. Save for a few headline-making outliers whose methodologies have been questioned by the scientific community, there's a large body of evidence that points to meat as a driver of disease. How-ever, looking closer at the data reveals an even more inter-esting picture: Rather than showing us a black-and-white absolute, the study indicates that there are ways to consume meat and reduce its harm.

Researchers have found that the way meat is prepared has a big impact on the risk it poses. Cooking meat at higher temperatures, for example, causes the fat to seep out and build up on hot cooking surfaces, creating polycyclic aromatic hydrocarbons (PAHs) that end up in the food. PAHs are a class of chemicals that occur naturally in coal, crude oil, and gasoline, so they're clearly not something you want a lot of in your food or your body. They've also been linked to a possible increased risk of certain cancers.

Quantity matters, too. Consuming larger quantities of red meat—especially the processed kind—has been repeatedly associated with a higher risk of type 2 diabetes, cardiovascular disease, and certain types of cancers (such as colon cancer), potentially due to nitrates present in these foods. Even the French government—in the country that created charcuterie—recently warned its citizens that cured meat consumption should be limited. And the World Health Organization (WHO) has even gone so far as to classify processed meats like ham, salami, bacon, and hot dogs as Group 1 carcinogens, a classification also held by asbestos, formaldehyde, and plutonium. Perhaps Doc Brown in *Back to the Future* could have powered the DeLorean with the contents of a charcuterie board and saved himself a lot of trouble. Alcohol is also in that group, which is telling. There's a societal norm we all embrace that alcohol is fine in moderation. As adults, we enjoy it with friends and family. Consuming it in small quantities generally doesn't lead to death. So perhaps we would be well served to think of meat in a similar fashion. Something that can be okay in smaller quantities, rather than as the 60 burgers the average American consumes each year.

There are some benefits to meat. Beef and chicken are high in omega-6 fatty acids, which are a key part of a well-rounded diet. But it's a delicate balance. We should strive to consume 1 to 4 times more omega-6 fatty acids than omega-3 fatty acids. But the typical American eats 11 to 30 times more omega-6 fatty acids than omega-3s. Many researchers feel that uneven ratio could be contributing to our skyrocketing inflammation disorders, a bracket term for issues ranging from diabetes, obesity, and cancer to irritable bowel syndrome (IBS), rheumatoid arthritis, lupus, and others. Meal plans like the

Mediterranean diet put omega-6 and omega-3 consumption back in balance by reducing intake of animal protein and replacing it with Power Five foods that have been proved to improve health over time.

There are other ways, too. Sourcing better-quality meat can also impact those numbers. Typical store-bought grain-fed beef has an omega-6 to omega-3 ratio of 9:1. But grass-fed beef has as much as four times the omega-3s, and its ratio is closer to 2:1. So what meat you choose really does matter.

SOURCING YOUR MEAT

While meat falls into the "eat less" category, it really should be "eat better." Here's a secret your doctor hasn't told you: Sourcing better meat is better for your health. And I'm about to tell you why.

Let's start by addressing the rise of plant-based meat products. The popularity of Beyond Meat and the Impossible Burger are an acknowledgment that eating more plants is something people *want* to do—and that's a good thing. We should be increasing our plant consumption and decreasing our meat intake for the benefits of our health and environment. However, the jury is still out on whether these manufactured plant-based foods are any better for us, healthwise. In my opinion, if you want to eat meat, you should eat the real thing. Just do it better by choosing higher-quality meat and eating it less frequently.

I became interested in where my food comes from in my 20s, even taking to the web to create a fun and informative series called *The Dairy Show (thedairyshow.com)*. I hit the road with a camera and started interviewing farmers, ranchers, and animal husbandry experts. I quickly learned these professionals really cared about the animals they raised, and I expanded my relationships with some of the best over the years.

I've come to know and respect Paul Willis, the founding hog farmer of Niman Ranch. Twenty-five years ago, when he started with Niman, small, pasture-based hog farmers were struggling to compete among the industrial livestock competitors dominating the industry. Paul wanted nothing to do with the hog factories that were springing up around his home in Iowa. His first five pigs were actually given to him for free with his purchase of a sow, which he says sounded like a good deal at the time. It turns out that sow would change the course of his life—and meat production as a whole. Paul's work impacted hundreds of ranchers who also wanted to raise animals cleanly, sustainably, and humanely.

"I enjoyed the animals being out on the pasture," Paul told me. "Our standards are based on the natural inclinations of the animals. They have to have bedding to nest and plenty of room." Paul's systems are based on Swedish methods, developed when confinement systems were outlawed there. "At the time, I wasn't raising pork chops; I was raising pigs."

After seeing free-range chicken labels start to pop up at grocery stores, Paul wondered if there was a market for pasture-raised pigs. He connected with Bill Niman and ended up selling pork to some of the most influential chefs in the country. "Bill told me Alice Waters of Chez Panisse loves it. I said, 'Who's that?'"

Paul and Bill found other farmers who were interested in raising animals more naturally and sustainably, and more chefs and regular folks signed on as customers. Today, Niman has a network of 750 family farmers, all committed to raising their animals with a high standard of care. Paul admits he had no idea what the Niman Ranch company would become when he started, and he takes pride in its grassroots beginnings. Paul's farm was the first in the United States to be Certified Animal Welfare Approved.

A few years ago, I attended the Niman annual Hog Farmer Appreciation Dinner in Des Moines, Iowa. At the dinner, famous chefs use Niman products to whip up an amazing meal to honor farmers. It was truly the "farmer prom" of my dreams and was actually incredibly moving. In a world where fewer children are following in their farming parents' footsteps, I met younger and older generations who work hand in hand to sustain the family business and the land at the same time. I saw more than a few tough dudes break down in tears during some of the presentations. These folks work really, really hard and rarely take a break. They take amazing pride in what they do and being part of Niman lets them farm better and live better all around.

GRASS-FED LABELS TO LOOK FOR

Certified Grassfed by AGW + Animal Welfare Approved: The original champion for the Animal Welfare Approved label and a good friend, Andrew Gunther, is unfortunately no longer with us, but this powerful program lives on. This label guarantees that beef was grass fed and finished with no grain and the animals lived a good life. It's one of the strongest animal welfare labels there is, and it's backed up with inspections.

American Grassfed Association (AGA) Certified: This is a meaningful label that verifies the beef was grass fed and finished. The AGA is a network of farmers who hold conferences filled with real cowboys coming together to further the cause over some great meals and (of course) delicious meats.

But the sad truth is most of the meat consumed in the United States is not from operations that meet Niman standards. The supermarket meat we buy and consume largely comes from industrial farms very far removed from what generations of ranchers know is the best way to rear animals. Factory-farmed meat keeps cows or hogs congregated in small quarters amid feces and bacteria. They eat on large feedlots or grow-out facilities designed to increase speed to market and increase the bottom line, not make a healthier animal.

I am not the first to point that out to you, and I won't be the last. But I will tell it to you straight: It's useless to fault corporate farms for trying to pump out more meat for less cost. As a society, consumers have been telling them for years that's what they want—quantity over quality. After all, eating meat two meals a day, seven days a week is the American way. We line up for new fast-food fried chicken sandwich launches the way we used to queue up for concert tickets. We come running at the promise of a steak as big as our head with a double coupon on Wednesdays. Watching another Netflix documentary showcasing the problem will do little to improve your health, but choosing better with your dollars sends a real signal to the meat industry. And decreasing the demand for commodity meat by making it a *sometimes* food rather than a default main could protect you from disease, lengthen your life, and leave you with a more varied palate that seeks out different flavors and textures.

I have learned one important golden rule when it comes to buying meat: How the animals are raised makes a difference in the final product. And if you eat meat less frequently, it's easier to afford paying a little more for better quality.

There are also a lot of strong arguments about the environmental impact of eating meat at the current volume we consume as a society. It's true livestock is responsible for releasing natural greenhouse gases into the atmosphere. But it's also important to note that industrialized nations' overconsumption of meat is largely driving the trend, along with the environmentally detrimental refrigeration and packaging that come with it. Interestingly, raising animals on pastures helps sequester carbon in the soil, restoring degraded land and helping secure farmland from droughts and heavy rain.

I firmly believe sustainable, local farming can create a harmonious ecosystem where the soil creates healthy plants, which feed healthier animals, which create manure to make healthier soil. And, somewhere in that circle is you, standing in a grocery store trying to decide what steak or chicken to buy to make you healthier. You may not be eager to throw on boots and waders and head out to a ranch, but you can develop a relationship with your local mom-and-pop butcher or even the butcher at your grocery store. That puts you one step closer to where your meat comes from. Better yet, finding a local farm or ranch and buying direct greatly reduces the ecological footprint of your next meal. Eating less meat that's of higher quality should be the goal we strive for.

THE CHICKEN-BUYING DANCE

In *The Power Five,* all the recipes with chicken call for whole chickens. I always buy whole chickens because it's less costly than buying chicken in parts. And that goes for producers too, because it turns out chickens are not so cheap to raise on a pasture. What's more, heirloom breeds take longer to grow and are at risk of being eaten by predators, which also ups the cost. I also believe buying chicken parts is treating a chicken like a commodity instead of honoring the bird. Data hasn't suggested that eating chicken is bad for your health, like other meats, but many of you want to cut back on meats as a whole, so if you are going to eat less, I want you to eat better and choose your bird wisely.

MEAT ME HALFWAY

Meat should always be lean and "rare," meaning *eaten rarely*. That's what's best for your health and the planet. But if you're going to eat it, you should eat it right. So I am giving you five of my favorite meat preparations for when you do want to indulge. While I generally keep a vegetable-forward diet, when I want a steak, I have one. And some would say when I have a steak, I don't mess around. In fact, I built an open-air fire pit grill, inspired by my love of traditional cooking methods, at my home. And there's nothing more long-established than cooking over a wood-burning fire—just ask any caveman. My grill was inspired by Patagonian chef Francis Mallmann, known the world over for his rustic cuisine. I use it to make bread, pizza, roasted cabbage, eggplant, and sometimes meat.

Whenever I am making meat, it's something I plan for. These recipes are not meant to be quickie meals, and instead rely heavily on dry brining to maximize the flavor and treatment of the precious muscle that you are cooking. Allowing your brined meat to sit in the refrigerator seals in the moisture and won't leave you with a dry, tough finished product that needs heavy or high-calorie sauces. In fact, brining your meat makes it harder to overcook and more foolproof; it honors the meat by maximizing its flavor.

The idea here is to make the Power Five foods the stars of your plate, and meat can be the garnish. Once you harness the tools to make fruits and vegetables, beans, whole grains, fish, and nuts and seeds with maximum flavor and textural impact, you will find yourself coming to this chapter less and less. That's what I mean by *"meat* me halfway"; it's not about compromising your diet by letting go of meat entirely if you don't want to. Instead, it's about expanding your culinary range so that meat isn't your fallback in meal planning.

CHICKEN LABEL DECODER

During my time with *Consumer Reports,* I was appointed by the secretary of agriculture to the U.S. Department of Agriculture's (USDA) National Advisory Committee on Meat and Poultry Inspection. Around once a year, I found myself in a room where representatives from cattle associations, poultry farms, government agencies, and consumer groups all gathered to discuss label regulations for meat that would eventually become your dinner. While most brought the best of intentions to the table, a lot goes into decisions about food packaging, and it's not always clear or even regulated. So here is a cheat sheet to help you navigate the labels you'll see the most.

Organic: Considered the gold standard of meaningful labels, this label means chickens are grown without antibiotics and have access to the outdoors. They also are organically fed.

Raised Without Antibiotics: The overuse of antibiotics in animals is a contributing factor to the rising threat of antibiotic resistance. This label means those drugs weren't given to the animals, but it doesn't tell you anything else about how they were raised.

Hormone Free: Raising chickens without hormones is already an established USDA regulation, so this is a meaningless label and isn't really a selling point for choosing one brand over another.

Natural: This is to denote that there are no artificial colorings or flavorings, but it is mostly a marketing tool and not a label to look for.

Free-Range: While this label conjures pastoral images of chickens pecking away as they frolic in green pastures, in order for poultry to qualify for this label, the animal simply needs access to an open area for a minimum of five minutes per day.

Pasture Raised: This means the chicken spends the majority of its day outdoors, but the use of the label is unregulated. Still, I always look for pasture-raised chicken and eggs.

Animal Welfare Approved: If you want happy chickens frolicking in a field, then this is what you want to look for. This label tells you how farms treat their chickens. Overseen by a nonprofit group, A Greener World (AGW), it is mostly given to small, independent farms that allow for continuous access to the outdoors. The animals are given a well-balanced, varied diet and the farm must agree to an annual inspection by AGW.

Heritage: This means the chicken hatched from an egg sired by an American Poultry Association Standard breed established before the mid-20th century. These birds tend to be slow growing and allowed to live until an older age, developing more flavor over time. They have much less breast meat and longer legs, and they're more costly to rear, which inflates the price you will see on the label.

Regenerative: This is a newer label started by the Rodale Institute and private companies with an ecological mission. It means the farm where the chicken was raised operates in a way that promotes long-term soil health and biodiversity. It is not government regulated.

Air-Chilled: Traditionally, chicken is doused with water to cool it down. Some claim the excess water evaporates out during the cooking process, drying out the meat, making it rubbery, and losing some of its natural flavor. Air-chilled chicken avoids the water bath, which some say makes the meat more juicy and delicious.

PORK SHOULDER STEAK WITH APPLE SALSA VERDE

When you think about grilling pork, you probably think about chops. I chose a shoulder steak to show you how to use more of the animal. This less expensive cut, usually associated with the long, slow cook of barbecue, is just as good if not better on the grill. It's dry brined to lock in moisture. Grilling pork adds a nice smokiness to its flavor, but you can also use a grill pan if you don't have access to an outdoor grill. Just cook the pork over high heat for 12 to 15 minutes or until a meat thermometer reads 145°F.

2½ to 3 pounds boneless pork shoulder, trimmed

Salt and pepper

Olive oil

Apple Salsa Verde (see recipe, page 220)

1. Cut the pork shoulder into 4 to 5 steaks, or ask your butcher to do it. While you are making the steaks, cut away any excess fat or connective tissue. Line a sheet pan with parchment paper, and top with a wire rack. Place the pork steaks on the rack, and season with salt and pepper. Place in the refrigerator until ready to cook (I recommend you do this in the morning or the night before).

2. Remove the pork from the fridge, and let it sit for 20 minutes while you preheat a grill to medium-high heat. When the grill is hot, rub the grate with oil, and cook the steaks, covered with the grill lid, 6 to 8 minutes per side or until nicely browned and a meat temperature inserted into thickest portion reads 145°F. Let rest for 5 to 10 minutes. Serve with Apple Salsa Verde.

APPLE SALSA VERDE

Salsa verde is one of my absolute favorite toppings for any of the Power Five foods and, of course, meat. This version adds apples for crunch. The main thing with salsa verde is to make it your own, so feel free to mix up the type and amount of herbs, use your choice of acid, and add nuts or seeds.

4 anchovies packed in olive oil, drained

2 tablespoons capers

2 cloves garlic, peeled

½ cup packed fresh basil leaves (scant ½ ounce)

½ cup packed fresh cilantro leaves (scant ½ ounce)

½ cup packed fresh Italian parsley leaves (scant ½ ounce)

1 teaspoon finely grated lemon zest

¼ cup lemon juice

1 cup extra-virgin olive oil

1 tart apple, cut into medium dice

¼ teaspoon (or more) dried crushed red pepper flakes

½ to ¾ teaspoon sea salt

1. Finely mince the anchovies, capers, and garlic (or use a food processor; I like to chop by hand to get more texture). Transfer to a medium bowl.

2. Coarsely chop the basil, cilantro, and parsley. Add to the bowl with the anchovy mixture. Stir in the lemon zest and juice. Gradually whisk in the olive oil. Add the apple. Season with red pepper flakes and sea salt.

CHICKEN IN VINEGAR

The technique of cooking chicken in vinegar is often attributed to chef Paul Bocuse, whose Poulet au Vinaigre is a French classic, but there are various versions from around the world. You can make this with only the red wine vinegar, and it will turn out just great. But if you want to meet your new favorite acid, do yourself a favor and purchase some ume plum vinegar, made of the liquid brine left over from pickling plums. It's sweet and bright and takes this chicken dish to the next level.

1 (3- to 4-pound) whole chicken

Kosher salt

¼ cup extra-virgin olive oil

5 cloves garlic, minced

2 red bell peppers, sliced

2 tomatoes, sliced (fresh or canned)

1 leek, sliced

1 fennel bulb, sliced

1 cup red wine vinegar

1 tablespoon ume plum vinegar

1. The Day Before Cooking: Line a sheet pan with parchment paper, and place a wire rack on top. Place the chicken on the rack on the sheet pan, and season generously with salt. Refrigerate, uncovered, overnight.

2. The Day of Cooking: Preheat the oven to 250°F. Cut the chicken into 6 to 8 pieces (2 legs, 2 thighs, and 2 to 4 breast pieces with wings).

3. Heat the oil in a sauté pan over medium-high heat. Cook the chicken, in batches with the skin sides down, in hot oil for 5 minutes per side or until browned. Transfer to a plate. Add the garlic, bell peppers, tomatoes, leek, and fennel to the pan, and cook for 5 minutes. Stir in the vinegars, and bring to a boil. Return the chicken to the pan, reduce the heat, and cook, covered, for 20 minutes. Uncover and cook for 5 minutes or until a meat thermometer inserted into the thickest portion of the thigh reads 165°F. Transfer the chicken to an oven-safe serving dish, and keep warm in the oven.

4. Continue cooking the sauce for 15 minutes or until reduced to 1 cup. Pour the sauce over the chicken, and serve immediately.

Spicy Scallion
Slaw (page 225)

Roasted Garlic
Chicken (page 224)

ROASTED GARLIC CHICKEN

I like dry brining chicken because it lets the spices penetrate inside and tenderizes the meat without the fuss and bulkiness of a wet brine. Spatchcocked chicken makes for a beautiful presentation and allows for even cooking, lessening the risk you'll end up with dried-out breasts.

1 (3- to 4-pound) whole chicken

Kosher salt

1 head garlic

Zest of 2 lemons

1 tablespoon finely chopped fresh rosemary

2 tablespoons extra-virgin olive oil

1. The Day Before Roasting: Line a sheet pan with parchment paper, and place a wire rack on top. Spatchcock the chicken by cutting out the backbone with a pair of kitchen shears. Open the chicken, and flatten the bird by pressing downward with the heel of your hand. (You will need to use some force.) Place the chicken on the rack on the sheet pan, and season generously with salt. Refrigerate, uncovered, overnight. Freeze the backbone to make stock, if desired.

2. The Day of Cooking: Preheat the oven to 350°F. Peel the outer husk from the garlic, but leave enough to keep the head intact. With a sharp knife, cut the top (stem end) off the garlic. Wrap the garlic head in aluminum foil. Roast for 30 to 45 minutes or until the cloves are soft when pressed. Let cool.

3. Stir together the roasted garlic, lemon zest, and rosemary to make a paste. Stir in the olive oil. Spread the paste over the chicken, and return to the refrigerator until ready to cook (1 to 8 hours ahead).

4. Place a cast-iron skillet or roasting pan large enough to hold the chicken in the oven, and preheat to 450°F for 30 minutes. Carefully place the chicken in the preheated skillet, and roast for 40 minutes to 1 hour (depending on the size of your bird) or until a meat thermometer inserted into the thickest portion of the thigh reads 165°F.

5. Let the chicken rest for 10 minutes. Carve the chicken into 6 to 8 pieces (2 legs, 2 thighs, and 2 to 4 breast pieces with wings).

ROASTED CHICKEN WITH SPICY SCALLION SLAW

In this recipe, after spatchcocking and roasting, the chicken gets topped with a slaw made of scallion greens, red peppers, Szechuan peppercorns, and sesame seeds, providing two Power Five foods—veggies and seeds—with your meat.

1 (3- to 4-pound) whole chicken

Kosher salt

Zest and juice of 1 lemon, divided

1 bunch scallions, greens only, very thinly sliced diagonally

1 red bell pepper, thinly sliced

¼ cup extra-virgin olive oil

1 teaspoon cracked Szechuan peppercorns

2 teaspoons sesame seeds

1. The Day Before Cooking: Line a sheet pan with parchment paper, and place a wire rack on top. Spatchcock the chicken by cutting out the backbone with a pair of kitchen shears. Open the chicken, and flatten the bird by pressing downward with the heel of your hand. (You will need to use some force.) Place the chicken on the rack on the sheet pan, and season generously with salt. Sprinkle lemon zest over chicken. Refrigerate, uncovered, overnight. Freeze the backbone to make stock, if desired.

2. The Day of Cooking: Remove the chicken from the fridge, and let it to come to room temperature.

3. Place a cast-iron skillet or roasting pan large enough to hold the chicken in the oven, and preheat the oven to 450°F for 30 minutes. Pat the chicken dry with a towel before it goes in the oven to remove any excess water. Carefully place the chicken in the preheated skillet, and roast for 40 minutes to 1 hour (depending on the size of your bird) or until a meat thermometer inserted into the thickest portion of the thigh reads 165°F.

4. Let the chicken rest for 10 minutes. Carve the chicken into 6 to 8 pieces (2 legs, 2 thighs, and 2 to 4 breast pieces with wings). Sprinkle the lemon juice over the chicken.

5. Combine the scallions, red pepper, olive oil, peppercorns, and sesame seeds. Just before serving, season with salt to taste. Serve the slaw with the chicken.

// THE MEATS

225

GRILLED GRASS-FED STEAK

A high-quality grass-fed steak can be expensive, but that's okay, because you are rarely going to eat one, and a little really goes a long way. And you will surely be serving lots of vegetables along with it. Make one big steak for a crowd and search out a thick cut, two inches or more. Slice it into strips and serve alongside the recipes in the earlier chapters, and people will be surprised how satisfied they are. You can also cook this in a grill pan until a meat thermometer reads 125°F.

1 (2-inch-thick) grass-fed bone-in New York strip, rib eye, or porterhouse steak

Salt

3 tablespoons rose harissa (store-bought or see recipe, page 29)

Olive oil

1. Two Days Before Cooking: Line a sheet pan with a piece of parchment paper, and top with a wire rack. Place the steak on the rack, and season thoroughly with salt. Refrigerate, uncovered, for 1 day.

2. The Day Before Cooking: Coat the steak evenly with the harissa. Refrigerate, uncovered, for another day.

3. The Day of Cooking: To cook the steak, prepare a grill for both indirect and direct cooking by building a fire on one side while leaving the opposite side unlit. Rub the grate over the fire with oil, and add the steak. Grill for 7 minutes on each side. Move the steak to the unlit side of the grill and, if possible, stand the steak up on its end. Grill, covered with the grill lid, for 40 minutes or until a meat thermometer reads 125°F to 130°F, turning the steak halfway through or if one side begins to cook too quickly. Remove from the grill, and let rest for 10 minutes. Slice and serve.

CHAPTER TEN

THE SWEETS

WHEN I WAS IN MEDICAL SCHOOL, there was a local speaker series featuring chefs held at a nearby cooking supply store. On a night with a huge blizzard bearing down on the city, famed chef David Bouley was giving a talk. I was not going to miss it, and, after much cajoling, I got my roommate Corey to drive me. We listened to Chef Bouley tell stories and share his passion for food and ingredients for hours. I was riveted and completely unfussed about just how much snow was accumulating outside the building (fortunately, Corey got us back to campus safely). This was David Bouley, after all! David Bouley of the eponymous Bouley restaurant (where 7,000 people surveyed by Zagat said they'd want to eat the last meal of their life!).

After his lecture, I stayed to say hello and maybe gush a little bit. To my surprise, Chef Bouley invited me to come work in the kitchen at his restaurant. I took him up on his offer, and my first day was rather interesting. Here I was, an out-of-place medical student with a hidden passion for cooking and baking, working among a top-notch kitchen staff. The head pastry chef was out that day, so I reported to Christina Tosi, now a culinary star in her own right as the founder of Milk Bar, the sister bakery to Momofuku, and celebrity host of several TV cooking shows. But back then she was mostly known as a behind-the-scenes genius, and that night she had *me* to figure out.

I wasn't getting paid in money, just experience, but I showed up early and was one of the last to leave at night. This wasn't about putting the gig on my résumé; I was there to learn. At first, most of the chefs, Christina included, didn't know what to make of me. But my eagerness won them over and, boy, did I get a hands-on education, which, oddly, I took right back with me to med school.

I have always found a way to hone the craft of cooking alongside my medical pursuits. At New York Medical College I asked the director of student activities if I could start a pastry club. He obliged and gave me a couple hundred dollars to get one going. It may sound contradictory—a bunch of doctors getting together to make sweets—but it got a lot of people interested in cooking and started some important conversations about sugar, diet, and how we find compromise in a healthy way. That very guidance, we came to find out, was a topic our patients would need from us just as much as a flick of the wrist on the prescription pad—probably more. And it was not being taught in the classroom. (I am happy to report that times have changed. Today, students at my alma mater have spearheaded a whole culinary medicine program, making sure medical students learn the importance of food and health.)

Years in academia learning how overindulging in sugar was making people sick, and seeing how much joy the sweet, delicate pastries I was making in the Bouley kitchen brought to people was something I had to reconcile. The light bulb moment came a few years later when I was studying public health and found data that shows total abstinence from things like sugar, in the form of yo-yo dieting, wasn't making people thinner or healthier over time. In fact, it was causing them to gain more weight in the long run. Every time they fell off the draconian diet wagon, they were left with a few extra pounds, which added up over a lifetime. It soon became clear to me that no one gets diabetes from eating birthday cake once a year. It's the unceremonious, mindless kind of eating over years and years that forms the habits that lead to disease. This is why sweets are our other "undeniable."

Baking appeals to my scientific side. You're weighing things and applying chemistry. The recipes in this book are born from that scientific approach; they use whole wheat flours and more whole fruits than traditional desserts. I've cut down on the sugar, though it's still there. And I make use of heart-healthy olive oil instead of butter. While I don't make dessert a habit, when I am going to have a dessert, I make sure it's worth it. I have taken my knowledge as a trained pastry chef and my doctorly scientific method to the kitchen to experiment with different flours, moisture levels, and baking times. You may be surprised to find these recipes don't include any chemical sugar alternatives. Be warned: These are not flavorless, Frankensteined, dietary versions of your favorite desserts.

What you *will* find is sourdough brownies (page 233) with a memorable herbal warmth from cardamom and a light kick from Urfa chile. You will discover a cheesecake (page 235) I perfected after a trip to Israel, where labneh is a way of life. Equally as satisfying as any New York–style cheesecake, it is light and tangy, and yet rich from the double-strained labneh. And then there are the four versions of my Three Seasons Cake (page 237) to help you celebrate produce at its peak, nature's most rhythmic little miracle. So go ahead, dive in and enjoy some sweets—with joy and intention.

CARDAMOM-URFA SOURDOUGH BROWNIES

Congratulations, you read through all the health information in this book and made it to the brownie recipe! If you skipped right to this page, I have bad news: These are "healthier" brownies. But once you try them, you'll forget all about that. Cardamom has an inviting flavor with a smoky, minty essence. The heat from the Urfa chile does a little dance with the sweet from the chocolate.

100 grams extra-virgin olive oil, plus more for the pan

½ tablespoon black cardamom seeds, toasted and crushed

½ teaspoon Urfa chile flakes (dried Turkish chile peppers)

549 grams bittersweet chocolate, chopped, divided

200 grams sugar

3 large eggs

150 grams sourdough starter (leftover, if desired; 75 grams whole wheat flour and 75 grams water)

1 teaspoon vanilla

½ teaspoon salt

1. Preheat the oven to 375°F. Wipe the bottom and sides of an 8-inch square pan with olive oil, and line with parchment paper. It's okay if the parchment paper extends over the top of the pan about an inch.

2. Place the cardamom seeds, Urfa chile, and 412 grams of chocolate in a heatproof bowl, and place over a pot of gently simmering water to create a double boiler. Gradually melt the chocolate together with the spices. When the chocolate is melted, stir in the olive oil, and let cool.

3. In an electric mixer fitted with the whisk attachment, beat the sugar and eggs at medium-high speed until pale and tripled in volume (this should take a solid 5 minutes). Beat in the starter, vanilla, and salt. Add the chocolate–olive oil mixture, and beat at medium speed until well combined (don't overmix), scraping the sides and bottom of the bowl as needed. Fold in the remaining 137 grams chopped chocolate, and scrape the batter into the prepared pan.

4. Bake for 50 minutes to 1 hour or until a wooden pick inserted into the center comes out mostly clean (the top of the brownies will have a little shine). Remove from the oven, and let cool completely. These brownies are very fudgy, so refrigerate once cooled, cut into squares while cold, and enjoy at room temperature.

// THE SWEETS

233

PREP TIME: 25 MINUTES   COOK TIME: 25 MINUTES

CHOCOLATE LABNEH CHEESECAKE

Labneh produces a lighter, fluffier cheesecake (in this case, crustless) than you've ever had. You can melt the chocolate and stir it into the batter for a smooth and creamy consistency, but I like to add it unmelted for crunch. Dark chocolate is full of important minerals, including iron, magnesium, zinc, copper, and phosphorus, which can be immunity building and help strengthen your bones. But its best component has to be flavonoids: powerful antioxidants that can reduce inflammation in your body and in turn lower your risk of heart disease and diabetes.

Olive oil

1 pound labneh (store-bought or see recipe, page 28)

½ cup sugar

3 large eggs

85 grams (3 ounces) dark chocolate, chopped

50 grams (¼ cup) whole wheat Kamut or einkorn flour

1. Preheat the oven to 400°F. Lightly coat the bottom and sides of a 6- or 7-inch springform pan with olive oil, and line the bottom and sides with parchment paper. Don't let the paper extend over the top of the pan.

2. Whisk together the labneh and sugar in a large bowl. Whisk in the eggs, chocolate, and flour. The flour may clump a bit, so you have to give it a vigorous whisking. Pour the batter into the prepared pan.

3. Bake for 25 to 30 minutes or until the top is browned (the center may not brown) and the cake is set on the sides but still has a little jiggle in the center. Let cool and unmold. Serve at room temperature, and store in the refrigerator.

CITRUS LABNEH CHEESECAKE: Omit the chocolate. Prepare the recipe as directed, stirring 2 tablespoons rose water and the zest of 1 orange into the batter with the eggs. Use true rose water, rather than essence or extract; it's more subtle. You don't want to bite into this and feel like you face-planted into a queen's garden. Think of it this way: Your partner doesn't want to have to overtly ask you to buy them flowers; they want you to do it on your own … after several low-key hints. But if you want to truly make them feel special, make them this cheesecake.

PREP TIME: 40 MINUTES   **COOK TIME:** 45 MINUTES

THREE SEASONS CAKE

This is based on a cake I learned to make during a cooking holiday in Le Marche, Italy. I call it a "three seasons" cake because you can make it with the fruits of spring, summer, and fall.

FOR THE CAKE

100 grams extra-virgin olive oil, plus more for greasing

200 grams whole wheat durum or Kamut flour

1 teaspoon baking powder

½ teaspoon salt

125 grams sugar

2 large eggs

1 teaspoon vanilla extract

SPRING: STRAWBERRY-RHUBARB FILLING

1 pound strawberries, whole (hulled) or halved, depending on size

1½ cups sliced rhubarb

1 tablespoon sugar

SUMMER: BLUEBERRY-APRICOT FILLING

1½ cups blueberries

Zest of 1 lemon

10 apricots, halved and pitted

SUMMER: PLUOT FILLING

10 pluots, halved and pitted

Ground cinnamon

FALL: MIXED BERRY FILLING

3 cups raspberries and blackberries

1. Preheat the oven to 350°F. If you're making the spring variation, combine the strawberries, rhubarb, and sugar in a bowl, and let stand 30 minutes. If you're making the first summer variation, combine the blueberries, zest, and apricots in a bowl.

2. Prepare the batter: Lightly coat an 8- or 9-inch cake or tart pan with olive oil, and place a parchment paper disc at the bottom of the pan.

3. Whisk together the flour, baking powder, and salt in a bowl. Beat the oil, sugar, eggs, and vanilla in the bowl of an electric stand mixer fitted with the paddle attachment until combined. Add the flour mixture and beat until just combined, scraping the bottom and sides of the bowl as needed. You will end up with a thick dough.

4. At this stage, stir either the strawberry-rhubarb mixture, blueberry-apricot mixture, pluots, or mixed berries into the dough. Scrape the dough into the prepared pan, and spread into an even layer. (You can also arrange the whole or halved fruit in a decorative pattern on top of the dough after adding the dough to the pan, if desired.) If you're making the second summer variation (with pluots), dust the top of the dough lightly with cinnamon.

5. Place the pan on a parchment paper–lined baking sheet. Bake for 45 to 55 minutes or until a paring knife inserted into the center comes out clean. Transfer to a cooling rack, and let cool. Remove from the pan, and serve.

PART FOUR

POWER PLAN YOUR MEALS

Armed with the Power Five foods and more than 85 recipes, it all comes down to incorporating these dishes into your meal planning. Here's a simple plan to make eating better a lifelong long-life habit.

CHAPTER ELEVEN

THE POWER PLAN

FOOD IS MORE THAN JUST SUSTENANCE. It's what we turn to for celebration—both in large gatherings and private moments. It's what we leave on the doorsteps of friends and family after they've suffered a tragic loss. It's medicine for your body *and* your soul. By this point in the book, you have learned how to harness the Power Five by unlocking the flavor and texture of whole, nutritious foods. Now I want to help you fit them into your everyday life.

THE 4/5 RULE

Here is a Power Plan strategy to maximize *The Power Five* to have the greatest impact on your health:

- **Every day, you should strive to eat from four of the Power Five food groups:**
  - The Fruits & Vegetables (chapter four)
  - The Beans (chapter five)
  - The Grains (chapter six)
  - The Fish (chapter seven)
  - The Nuts & Seeds (chapter eight)
- **Once a week, you should hit all of the Power Five food groups in a single day.**
- **Cook for a crowd even if you're alone:** I seek out opportunities to cook for a crowd whenever I can. But even if I plan to eat alone, I make a large quantity of what I'm cooking and multiple sides, because leftovers today mean a stress-free tomorrow. It's a simple way to automate your diet for the week, mixing and matching as you go.
- **Power up your Power Five:** In my book *What to Eat When,* I lay out the science behind eating according to your circadian rhythms, hearkening back to a time before electric light, when our bodies were in tune with the sun and moon cycles. The "When Way" of eating calls for you to eat your largest meal of the day first and your smallest meal last, and to fast after the sun sets. This creates a natural intermittent fasting period that mostly happens while you're asleep, so it's easier to maintain and can help you lose weight.
- **Ditch the meal labels:** Who says one thing is a breakfast food and another is a dinner? From my exploration of culture and cuisines around the world, I've learned that associating partic-ular kinds of foods with a certain time of day is very much influenced by where we live. In the United States, we think of cereal, pancakes, and pastries as breakfast foods, but in other parts of the world, breakfast can be salad, vegetables, and fish. So don't be afraid to try eating *The Power Five* recipes at any time of day.

THE ESSENTIAL POWER FIVE STAPLES SHOPPING LIST

Keep these ingredients in your refrigerator and pantry and you'll be set to make *The Power Five* recipes at a moment's notice.

Oils
- Your favorite high-quality extra-virgin olive oil for finishing
- Extra-virgin olive oil for cooking

Spices (store spices in the fridge to prolong freshness)
- Sea and kosher salts
- Black peppercorns for grinding (The Reluctant Trading Experiment sells a black pepper that made me love black pepper)
- Za'atar
- Smoked paprika
- Sumac
- Urfa chile flakes
- Cobanero chile flakes

Canned and Jarred
- Heirloom beans
- Chickpeas
- Artichokes
- Tahini
- Peppadew peppers
- Rose harissa

Produce
- Garlic
- Lemons
- Fresh herbs

Whole Grains and Nuts
- Ancient grain whole wheat flours
- Whole wheat pasta (from Italy if possible)
- California walnuts
- Oats
- Freekeh
- Buckwheat

Dairy
- Labneh

Supplies

- Parchment paper
- Microplane grater
- Mandoline
- Cheesecloth
- Bamboo skewers

YOUR POWERED-UP MEAL PLAN

Figuring out what to make for breakfast, lunch, and dinner can be a daunting daily task. Even more so when you're looking to the week ahead. To get in the daily habit of eating the Power Five foods, I've created an easy week-long meal plan to get you started (with the Power Five categories in parentheses). Follow this plan, add your favorite recipes from this book, then modify your menu week to week.

Sunday

- Roasted Cone-Shaped Cabbage (fruits & vegetables)—page 91
- Smoky Eggplant With Hummus (nuts & seeds, fruits & vegetables, beans, and grains)—page 196
- Ancient Grain Whole Wheat Sourdough Focaccia (grains and fruits & vegetables)—page 136
   Note: This bread will last you all week. Start the recipe on Saturday and save enough spent starter for use Monday and Wednesday.
- Grilled Stone Fruit With Labneh and Basil (fruits & vegetables) —page 55

Monday

- Green Beans With Walnut Sauce (fruits & vegetables and nuts & seeds)—page 195
- Ancient Grain Whole Wheat Sourdough Focaccia (grains and fruits & vegetables)—page 136
   Note: Use some of the spent starter from Sunday
- Chickpea Murphy (beans and fruits & vegetables)—page 107

Tuesday

- Pink Fennel Salad (fruits & vegetables and nuts & seeds)—page 57
- Freekeh With Broccolini and Apricots (grains and fruits & vegetables)—page 159

- Beans Cooked Like Fish (beans, fruits & vegetables, and nuts & seeds)—page 113

Wednesday
- Raw Asparagus Salad (fruits & vegetables and nuts & seeds) —page 69
- Olive Oil–Poached Steelhead Trout (fish and fruits & vegetables) —page 178
- Mushroom Toast (grains, fruits & vegetables, and nuts & seeds) —page 145
  > Note: Keep using that whole wheat sourdough bread!

Thursday
- Roasted Oysters With Corn Butter (fish and fruits & vegetables) —page 181
- Fideo Paella (grains, fruits & vegetables, and beans)—page 153

Friday
- Roasted Harissa Carrots With Carrot-Top Pesto and Avocado (fruits & vegetables and nuts & seeds)—page 85
- Roasted Chicken With Spicy Scallion Slaw (fruits & vegetables and nuts & seeds)—page 225
- Beans and Greens (beans and fruits & vegetables)—page 110
- Three Seasons Cake (fruits & vegetables and grains)—page 237

Saturday
- Poached Leek Salad With Sunchokes (fruits & vegetables and nuts & seeds)—page 73
- Sumac Semi-Cured Slow-Roasted Steelhead Trout (fish)—page 174
- Sourdough Busiate With Trapanese-Style Pesto (grains, fruits & vegetables, and nuts & seeds)—page 157

NOW, LET'S PARTY! FIVE BOARDS YOUR GUESTS WILL NEVER GET BORED OF

If you noticed the beautiful and eye-catching butter boards that took over social media or are just looking for a new idea outside of the classic cheese board, I created five boards based on the Power Five foods that will make you and your guests want to graze for days. I love the idea of being artistic with food and culinary presentation, and I collect large, unique serving boards of all types from artisans and flea markets as the perfect blank canvas for me to be free and creative. I must warn you, however, if you show up to a party with one of these boards, be ready to accept a whole lot of fanfare and an assault of compliments. Introverts beware.

The Fruits & Vegetables: Use the Roasted Pepper Sauce (page 79) as a base, smoothing the sauce around the bottom of a cheese board. It's thick enough to spread, and it makes a bright, cheery base for you to top with edible flowers. Top the sauce with grilled vegetables (asparagus, radicchio, eggplant, and artichokes) for a veg-on-veg party starter that's as much a feast for the eyes as for the belly.

The Beans: Hummus beats butter on a board, hands down. You can use store-bought hummus, make your own (page 196), or make my Fave e Cicoria (page 109). Dunk the back of your spoon in the dip and drag it down the board to make little painterly dabs. Then, sprinkle lemon zest and a drizzle of extra-virgin olive oil on top. Serve with Ancient Grain Whole Wheat Sourdough Focaccia (page 136), cucumber spears, and carrots for dipping.

The Grains: Using labneh (page 28) as the base, make artistic dollops along an entire cheese board with the back of a spoon. Sprinkle tiny cubes of cucumber, tomato, and kalamata olives like confetti across the top. Or go the sweet route with crushed pistachios, pomegranate seeds, and mint, with a honey drizzle. Hit the whole thing with fresh cracked pepper and plate Ancient Grain Whole Wheat Sourdough Focaccia (page 136) and sliced peppers around the edges for dipping.

The Fish: Be the first on your block to make a fish board and school everyone on how to live your best life. Start with spreading Trout "Rillettes" (page 179) in a nice even layer on the board. Sprinkle capers, lemon zest, parsley, chopped tomatoes, and za'atar on top. Garnish with toasted slices of Pane di Staatsburg (page 138), sliced peppers, and cornichons for dipping.

The Nuts & Seeds: Start by lining your board with Mixed Nut Butter (page 35). Then take a knife and make fun swirls across the board in all different directions to create any pattern you like. Sprinkle on some dark chocolate cacao morsels, muddled strawberries, and coconut flakes. Serve with Whole Wheat Pane di Staatsburg (page 140) and let your inner child marvel at how far you've come from your PB&J days.

CONNECT WITH THE POWER

FOOD IS A POWERFUL CONNECTOR OF PEOPLE—a fact never as apparent to me as in the days after 9/11. My family and I were living in Battery Park City at the time, just blocks away from the World Trade Center. Those weeks after the tragedy were formative in my life. I saw my notoriously aloof fellow New Yorkers rally together in an almost unrecognizable way. Strangers would have meaningful conversations on the street, on barstools, and across tables at restaurants. It was as if we were all just trying to clutch on to something real in the face of what still felt unbelievable.

It was then that I found myself out to dinner at Palma, an Italian restaurant in Manhattan's Greenwich Village. Just days before, the Twin Towers would have been visible from the streets of the Village, soaring above the low-rise buildings that dominate this part of the city. But on that night, there was an empty space in the skyline as my mother and I sat at a table near the window, hungry. Very hungry.

In through the door came a jovial man with a single loaf of bread under his arm. My famished mother called out to him, "Hey, give us some of that bread." Looking back, it seems strange, but in the moments of those September days in 2001, our shock and newfound camaraderie made us bold.

He laughed and came over to our table, handed us some bread, and sat down. The friendly stranger introduced himself as Walter Luque, the head pastry chef for Palma and their catering kitchen down the block. Walter ended up having dinner with us, and as someone with a budding interest in culinary arts, I hung on to his every word. Walter invited me to come cook in the catering kitchen, and, of course, I was game.

Around 6 a.m. on a Saturday morning, the usually crowded streets of the Village are empty and peaceful, and for many months I found myself on them at this early hour, making my way to the kitchen. Once there, I was given a station and put largely in charge of prep work, aka grunt work, which I was happy to do in exchange for experience. I did a lot of chopping and dicing and peeling (especially baby carrots, baby artichokes, and snap peas). This was not glamorous work (though, not to brag, I *was* put in charge of Naomi Campbell's fruit salad once). Then one day, after I guess I had put in enough time to show my commitment, Walter told me it was time for me to work with him on pastries. We made glorious things together, including giant chocolate sculptures and even Howard Stern's birthday cake!

Walter and I became friends. He took me out to try foods at restaurants all over New York, where, despite usually having a small table, we would often order the whole menu so we could learn about new flavors and new ideas. He introduced me to other chefs, like the amazing Sue Torres, whose passion for Mexican cuisine and its regional variations excited both my taste buds and my intellect. He took me to supply shops only chefs knew about, like JB Prince, so I could be armed with the right cooking tools and cookware, but no extra gadgets that just lead to extra cleaning. And he took me to the cookbook store Kitchen Arts & Letters and helped me begin my own cookbook collection, which is now rather large. Walter made the world of cooking and baking, something that always felt out of reach, accessible and attainable. And it all started with a connection over a meal and some *really* good bread.

That connection with Walter inspired so many more. I've met and befriended countless farmers, ranchers, and other food artisans. I've learned from chefs and teachers, like Silvestro Silvestori at The Awaiting Table cooking school in Puglia, who by teaching people the traditional foodways of the region lives his dream life every day. My visit to Silvestro's school inspired me to follow my own dreams and passions, and he's also become a lifelong friend. All of these relationships have made my life richer and my love for food and cooking stronger.

So I hope that your cooking journey helps you make connections. I wish for you to be on a first-name basis with your butcher and to have a cheese guy or girl. I hope you find a favorite vendor at the farmers market who knows what kind of tomatoes you like. More than anything, I hope you share your cooking at large tables filled with family and friends and that the meal is accompanied by stories that induce laughter that echoes through your kitchen hours after the last plate is cleaned. I hope you find a Walter, who shows you a cookbook is a door to possibilities that can change your life. And I hope it is a long life.

ACKNOWLEDGMENTS

"NOTHING IN THIS WORLD is accomplished without passion." At least, that's what the small slip of paper I once extracted from a cookie and stuffed in my wallet said. For years, the paper and those words remained tucked between bills, credit cards, and the occasional quarter until it eventually disintegrated, but the message is still with me.

I have many passions, but the greatest are my mission to make the world a healthier place, where people live longer, and my love of creating joyous food that makes our lives worth living. I consider myself incredibly fortunate to find fulfillment pursing both at the same time.

People often ask me how I got into cooking, and the answer is simple: my mom. Some of my earliest memories are of making cookies with my mother when I was a toddler, her hands guiding my little fingers as we created meticulous little wonders out of some eggs, flour, butter, and sprinkles. From those early lessons, I was hooked for life. Both my parents taught me that food is health and always encouraged me to pursue my passion for it, even with the side effect of a huge mess in our kitchen. My dad deserves some credit, too. He raised me to understand that food and health go together, and while I was in college, he admonished me not to "skimp on food," which I took to mean eat out and learn a lot.

I love to cook and I love to eat, and, for me, these activities are acts of creativity, appreciation, and community. I cook most days, even when I travel (which is most days, lately). While on the road, I stay with friends and prepare meals in their homes, exploring new ingredients from local markets and taking time to be inspired by the local cuisine. I am thankful for all my friends who have invited me into their kitchens, dined with me, and lifted their glasses to meet mine in celebration—especially my college and med school buddies Andy (and his partner, Mari, and sous chef, Bea) and Corey (and his wife, Liz, and the best kitchen assistants there are: Hannah and Haley). I have deep gratitude for their indulging my need to visit many farmers markets and to stuff their kitchens with produce and "the right" pans and dishes.

Honestly, writing a cookbook is not something I thought I would ever do—again! (FYI: I am also passionate about exclamation points!) As much as I love cooking, writing a cookbook is hard work, and it truly takes a village. So I want to acknowledge the team at National Geographic. First, for asking me to write this book, and second, for helping me make it a true expression of myself. And last, for making these pages beautiful and fun to read. My senior editor, Allyson Johnson, was a great coach and ally; I thank project editor Ashley Leath for amazing attention to detail in editing the recipes; and my thanks also go to senior production editor Michael O'Connor, creative director Elisa Gibson, and lead designer Sanaa Akkach, whom I credit with lifting the aesthetics on every page within this binding to a place I could've only dreamed of when we started.

Photographs are one of the most important elements of a cookbook. They bring the recipe to life, and they're how many people decide to buy a book (I know I do). It turns out that creating the art for a cookbook takes yet another village and is a highly collaborative process. When we were working on *The What to Eat When Cookbook,* it took a long time to choose the perfect photographer. I passed on most of the options that were presented, but finally we found the one in Scott Suchman. Scott's passion shows through his work, and along with his passion for parchment paper, he is a master of lighting, makes food look exciting, and is fun to work with. I feel lucky to have had him photograph the recipes for both books and to have become friends. I am also thankful for Scott's assistant, Travis Marshall, who kept shoot days moving and whose keen eye made sure all the photos were perfect. In order to take photographs of recipes, you also need the food, and that's where the amazing Lisa Cherkasky and her assistant, Carolyn Robb, came in. Lisa trained as a chef at the Culinary Institute of America near my house in upstate New York, worked in some of the most hard-core kitchens, and now makes food look beautiful for newspapers, magazines, and books. When creating the recipes for this book, I thought a lot about how they would look (except for the fish baked in tahini sauce, which is delicious but not camera friendly), and

Lisa and Carolyn executed that vision and made them somehow look even better. It turns out that no cookbook photo shoot is complete without a backdrop, and I have to acknowledge the amazing work of Kristi Hunter, our set designer, who has an incredibly large dish collection that matched my style and made me extremely envious.

Of course, someone has to keep this team in line and follow through after the shoot, and for that I want to thank the brilliant National Geographic photo team, made up of director of photography Adrian Coakley, senior photo editor Jill Foley, and photo editor Katie Dance. They made sure the pictures in this book were perfect and not a speck of cilantro was out of place.

I also want to thank my recipe tester, Ashley Archer. Ashley is a TV producer, showrunner, recipe developer, food stylist, and incredible chef. Ashley has found a way to share her acumen in the culinary arts with the world in such a way that leaves the person (or millions of people, in the cases of her successful television shows) lucky enough to be receiving her wisdom inspired and empowered. Her rich experience in the restaurant world, along with her work in media and publishing, has made her a sought-after talent by some of the best known chefs in the world. I was lucky enough to get the chance to work with her because of sheer luck, as we were office neighbors at a production company. Her special touch is all over these pages, and my appreciation could fill a whole other book.

And last but not least, a huge thank-you to Kathy Gulinello, a great friend I was lucky to work side by side with for seven years, creating award-winning television programming on food and health. Kathy is a successful media professional, writer, and, as you've already read, the inspiration for my Pink Fennel Salad. She is also the most creative person I know. A blank page for Kathy is an opportunity, a chance to weave story and knowledge together with imagination and finesse. She embodies the words on that fortune cookie paper I got years before I ever met her, because she brings passion to everything she does. Kathy's knowledge of food, health, and me helped make this book worth reading.

KITCHEN SOURCES

SPICES

Like many people in the United States, I was raised in a home with a cabinet full of dusty, underused spices that were less than inspiring. But then I was awoken from the expired-jar doldrums, and it turns out there are countless peppercorn varieties to try, and oregano has varieties that are unique to their regions. Don't even get me started on chile pepper flakes, which come in a vast variety of flavors and colors. So as you use this book, consider waking up your cupboard with fresh, potent, and exciting spices, and keep trying new ones. Buy in small quantities, and, if you have the space, try storing your spices in the refrigerator to prolong their freshness.

Burlap & Barrel

This is a great place for get mail-order spices. I like their commitment to small farmers around the world and their attention to flavor and quality. *burlapandbarrel.com*

La Boîte

This is a favorite source for spices for some of New York City's greatest chefs. In addition to high-quality individual spices, they also have great mixes. Owner Lior Lev Sercarz has written multiple books on spices. I love visiting their store in Hell's Kitchen; it's a great place to discover new flavors and buy dried rose petals. *laboiteny.com*

SOS Chefs

This incredible store in New York City's East Village neighborhood has been spicing up the culinary scene for more than 25 years. A visit here is a great treat for the senses, and it is an amazing place to discover things you've never heard of. *sos-chefs.com*

FISH

My friend Silvestro Silvestori suggests thinking about the freshness of seafood in terms of the number of *hours* it has been out of the water—not days. It's a good rule to follow. Find a local place where you can get the freshest catch.

Hudson Valley Fisheries

For me, this is the freshest and highest-quality fish I can get where I live. They also ship overnight. *hudsonvalleyfisheries.com*

MEAT

Find a local farmer, visit, ask questions, and build a relationship with someone who raises animals the ways we discuss in the book. For a national supplier, there are our friends at Niman. You can read all about their farmers and standards at *nimanranch.com*.

BEANS

Rancho Gordo

Rancho Gordo doesn't just supply the best heirloom beans; they are also strongly committed to the welfare and livelihood of those who grow them. You can find Rancho Gordo beans in many specialty markets, as well as online. *ranchogordo.com*

GRAINS/FLOURS/SEEDS

Breadtopia

Breadtopia is my number one source for flour and bread-baking supplies. They have the biggest selection of whole wheat flours and grind them fresh to a perfect consistency. *breadtopia.com*

Bob's Red Mill

Bob's Red Mill is a great source for grains, seeds, and flours, as well as blanched fava beans. *bobsredmill.com*

PASTA

Once upon a time, whole wheat pasta wasn't very tasty. Cooking it resulted in something mushy or gummy that just didn't compare with white flour–based pastas. But those days are gone. Now there are many high-quality whole wheat pastas on the market. You can find these online or at specialty stores like Eataly.

Benedetto Cavalieri

The Cavalieri family has been making pasta for more than 100 years in a town called Maglie in southern Puglia, Italy. I've visited their factory and talked to the owner about the process they go through to create a super-high-quality whole wheat pasta. It took many years to find the right wheat and drying times, but the results are worth it. *benedettocavalieri.it*

Afeltra

This Campania, Italy–based pasta company makes a wide variety of organic whole wheat pasta shapes that come in a distinct red package. *pastificioafeltra.it*

Mancini Pastificio Agricolo

This company in Le Marche, Italy, cultivates their own wheat, which they turn into excellent whole wheat pastas. *pastamancini.com*

DISHES/SERVEWARE

Making food look beautiful includes how you bring it to the table. When you put your heart into cooking, you should also present the results of those efforts on a dish or serving piece that someone else also put their heart into.

L'impatience

These beautiful ceramics with a modern sensibility are made by a French husband and wife team who now live near me in upstate New York. *limpatience.com*

Noble Plateware

Wynne Noble started making handmade dishes in Brooklyn in 1985 for restaurants all around the world. I am lucky enough to have a few sets. Unfortunately, Wynne passed away a few years ago, but her legacy and style live on in the brand. *nobleplateware.com*

Heath Ceramics

Heath is one of the most iconic ceramic makers in California. When you go to a good restaurant in San Fran, chances are that the name Heath can be found *under* you meal. They have an amazing selection of shapes and colors. *heathceramics.com*

METRIC CONVERSIONS

The recipes in this book were developed using standard U.S. measures. The charts below offer equivalents for U.S. and metric measures. All conversions are approximate and have been rounded up or down to the nearest whole number.

WEIGHT CONVERSIONS

ounces	grams
½	14
¾	21
1	28
1½	43
2	57
2½	71
3	85
3½	99
4	113
4½	128
5	142
6	170
7	198
8	227
9	255
10	283
12	340
16 (1 pound)	454

VOLUME CONVERSIONS

U.S.	metric
1 teaspoon	5 milliliters
2 teaspoons	10 milliliters
1 tablespoon	15 milliliters
2 tablespoons	30 milliliters
¼ cup	59 milliliters
⅓ cup	79 milliliters
½ cup	118 milliliters
¾ cup	177 milliliters
1 cup	237 milliliters
1¼ cups	296 milliliters
1½ cups	355 milliliters
2 cups (1 pint)	473 milliliters
2½ cups	591 milliliters
3 cups	710 milliliters
4 cups (1 quart)	0.946 liter
1.06 quarts	1 liter
4 quarts (1 gallon)	3.8 liters

OVEN TEMPERATURES

Fahrenheit	225	250	275	300	325	350	375	400	425	450	475
Celsius	105	120	135	150	165	80	190	200	220	230	245
gas mark	¼	½	1	2	3	4	5	6	7	8	9

INDEX

Boldface page numbers indicate illustrations.

ILLUSTRATIONS CREDITS

All photographs by Scott Suchman except for page 16 by Nataša Mandić/Stocksy and page 22 by Trinette Reed/Stocksy. Food styling by Lisa Cherkasky. Prop styling by Kristi Hunter.

ABOUT THE AUTHOR

Michael Crupain, M.D., M.P.H., is a board-certified preventive medicine physician. He is the co-author of the national bestseller *What to Eat When* and *The What to Eat When Cookbook*. Dr. Crupain has had a unique career path, first training to be a neurosurgeon, then switching to preventive medicine. He has served as part-time faculty at the Johns Hopkins Bloomberg School of Public Health, hosted the farm-to-table cooking video blog *The Dairy Show*, served as director of food safety testing at *Consumer Reports*, was the medical director at *The Dr. Oz Show*, and is the executive vice president of clinical services at Sharecare. He has trained with top chefs in New York and at cooking schools, and he is a constant student of culinary traditions from around the world. The theme that connects all of Dr. Crupain's work is his mission to make the world a healthier, more delicious place to live.

Since 1888, the National Geographic Society has funded more than 14,000 research, conservation, education, and storytelling projects around the world. National Geographic Partners distributes a portion of the funds it receives from your purchase to National Geographic Society to support programs including the conservation of animals and their habitats.

Get closer to National Geographic Explorers and photographers, and connect with our global community. Join us today at nationalgeographic.org/joinus

For rights or permissions inquiries, please contact National Geographic Books Subsidiary Rights: bookrights@natgeo.com

Library of Congress Cataloging-in-Publication Data
Names: Crupain, Michael, author.
Title: The power five : a cookbook : essential foods for optimum health / Michael Crupain, M.D., M.P.H.
Description: Washington, D.C. : National Geographic, [2023] | Includes bibliographical references and index. | Summary: "This cookbook focuses on the five foods that will keep you living your best life - without sacrificing flavor"-- Provided by publisher.
Identifiers: LCCN 2023003980 (print) | LCCN 2023003981 (ebook) | ISBN 9781426222412 (hardcover) | ISBN 9781426222696 (ebook)
Subjects: LCSH: Cooking (Natural foods) | Natural foods. | Nutrition. | Diet. | Health. | LCGFT: Cookbooks.
Classification: LCC TX741 .C78 2023 (print) | LCC TX741 (ebook) | DDC 641.3/02--dc23/eng/20230210
LC record available at https://lccn.loc.gov/2023003980
LC ebook record available at https://lccn.loc.gov/2023003981

ISBN: 978-1-4262-2241-2

Printed in China

23/LPC/1